"At the ARF, we have proven that 'advertising works' over the course of the past 80 years. Today's marketers and their insight leaders need new solutions—at scale, and at the speed of life, at their fingertips. In Ad-itude, experienced leader Peter Daboll helps to articulate and explicate today's issues and opportunities. He brings forward solutions to answer the C-suite question: 'Do my marketing dollars drive growth' and 'where should I spend my next marketing dollar.' Today's big data analytics open up new possibilities of immediate access to competitive context, and real time insight aided by leaders with new skills: synthesis, speed vs. perfection, and the leadership to take a stand. Ace Metrix is one of many solutions the industry counts on to drive growth."

Gayle Fuguitt
CEO and president of *The Advertising Research Foundation*

USING DATA TO INSPIRE
EXTRAORDINARY AD CREATIVE

by Peter Daboll

Published by Advantage, Charleston, South Carolina.
Member of Advantage Media Group.

ADVANTAGE is a registered trademark and the Advantage colophon is a trademark of Advantage Media Group, Inc.

Printed in the United States of America.

ISBN: 978-1-59932-564-4
LCCN: 2015940055

Advantage Media Group is proud to be a part of the Tree Neutral® program. Tree Neutral offsets the number of trees consumed in the production and printing of this book by taking proactive steps such as planting trees in direct proportion to the number of trees used to print books. To learn more about Tree Neutral, please visit www.treeneutral.com. To learn more about Advantage's commitment to being a responsible steward of the environment, please visit www.advantagefamily.com/green

Advantage Media Group is a publisher of business, self-improvement, and professional development books and online learning. We help entrepreneurs, business leaders, and professionals share their Stories, Passion, and Knowledge to help others Learn & Grow. Do you have a manuscript or book idea that you would like us to consider for publishing? Please visit advantagefamily.com or call 1.866.775.1696.

To Karen:

*The love of my life who has made me the luckiest man on earth.
Constantly changing, never ending, connected to everything,
My everything, always.*

And to Cam, Giverny, and Michael:

Always keep reaching and you will change the world.

I have learned that it is far easier to write a speech (or a book) about good advertising than it is to write a good ad.

—Leo Burnett

FOREWORD

Being a marketer today is equal parts exhilaration and exhaustion. We have never had more access to information about consumers and their purchase journeys. We finally have dashboards that show how our marketing activities are actually translating into sales. We have new channels to learn, new metrics to master, new technologies to deploy. In all the conversations about disruption, however, one thing remains true—it is the marketer's job to connect with our consumers and customers and show them how our brand helps improve lives. As much as ever, succeeding in that task requires the emotional bond that great creative can deliver.

Peter has spent much of his life studying how and why some advertisements move the needle and others fall short. In *Ad-itude* he takes those lessons and shows us how we can be better. Through extensive analysis and case studies from some of the world's most respected brands, he demonstrates how marketers can create advertising that consumers want to watch and even share. He doesn't lean on formulas or simplistic platitudes but champions a test-and-learn attitude and new, real-time analytics. His advice will help marketers go beyond measuring and reporting outcomes to actually optimizing advertising creative and impacting business results.

For anyone who loves great advertising, *Ad-itude* provides an optimistic road map for the future.

Cammie Dunaway,
Former CMO Yahoo!, Nintendo, and KidZania

TABLE OF CONTENTS

SAME AS IT EVER WAS

The role of great creative in advertising has come full circle since the *Mad Men* days of the '50s and '60s when TV was new and ad creative ruled the airwaves. Over the past few years, creative has often taken a back seat to targeting and efficiency priorities in campaigns, especially in digital ones. But with more and more precise targeting, marketers are realizing that reach and efficiency alone aren't very persuasive. Once I find my ideal consumer, what should I say to them? How do I make them *feel* something? Great creative is differentiating. Everyone can use the same tools to buy and deliver a message efficiently. But in an era when consumers can just as easily avoid watching an ad, what is it that will make them pay attention at all? It's all about the creative.

Of course, great creative never really lost its impact; it was often deemed as a given—but less important than delivery variables. This was especially true with banner ads, with the format not lending itself too much creative differentiation. But, I think, in large degree, this happened because it was harder to measure creative impact than other marketing elements, so it was more difficult to clearly prove its value. And we tend to focus on things we can measure more easily. But doing something because it's easier doesn't make it right. What was required was a new paradigm (yes, I too hate that word) in measuring advertising effectiveness.

This book is about systematically measuring the effectiveness of video ad creative for every ad. This is an idea that inspired the company, Ace Metrix®, which fuels much of the data contained within these pages and one that was initially maligned by creatives but is now embraced. Ace Metrix is not the only solution for evaluating creative impact, but it is an important piece of the puzzle.

How do I know so much about Ace Metrix? Because I'm the CEO of the company. While findings from Ace Metrix research are the foundation for much of what I write about in this book, my experience in measuring creative effectiveness dates far back from before 2007, when Ace Metrix was founded. Back in the '80s I was part of IRI, the first company to use retail scanner data and targeted TV messages to create BehaviorScan®. Until recently, BehaviorScan represented one of the purest ways to test TV creative and media weight or other marketing variables. In today's world, it just became too slow. From there, I worked with other talented analysts to create some of the first marketing mix models, with many of the techniques still used today. This long (too long) history in marketing analysis shaped much of the direction for creative evaluation that is discussed in these chapters.

What has changed since I began this career in the '80s? Many things of course but chief among them are that marketers are now required to be technologists and data scientists who collect, understand, manage, and act on data in real time, in addition to their important role as strategists. Creative development, media execution (both TV and digital), and measurement are now intertwined and inseparable for marketers. But one thing that hasn't changed, and will not change, is the importance of the creative itself.

But how do we talk about creative in the context of data analytics? I'd like to think this book will be the Rosetta Stone between the artistic/creative side and the data/analytics side of the house. It's not a book about the creative use of data; it is a book about the use of creative data: data collected at unprecedented scale, specifically to quantify the quality and impact of the ad creative itself: not evaluating how *creative* the ad is but rather measuring how *successful* the ad creative is and quantifying its impact on viewers. Sometimes an ad that is considered highly creative may not be successful in achieving a brand's objective or vice versa.

Creative teams can now focus on massive experimentation and iterative testing to know how and why their ad works in driving business results as they are being created. That is a key theme of the book. Marketers should embrace real-time experiments to quantify and fine-tune their communication strategy. Despite the growth and popularity of various ROI and attribution models and predictive tools, there is no substitute for testing to isolate specific effects in current conditions. Models can produce wildly different results compared with the real world because of a blind spot or false assumptions. The current state of the art for predictive models is far from perfect, yet models are often billed as such, and it is my belief that many marketers, who rely too heavily on marketing mix models or other forms of prediction, are setting themselves up for failure. There are times when making decisions based on a "hard" return-on-investment (ROI) number from a holistic mix model is actually riskier than an educated guess, once you understand how that predictive model is constructed. Digital data streams have exacerbated this problem. I'm reminded of a concept fostered for years in a quote attributed to John Maynard Keynes: "I'd rather be vaguely right than precisely wrong." Yet, today, there is an alternative. There is an unprecedented opportunity for inexpensive, real-time experimentation or testing that often isn't fully exploited. A marketer's job should be one of a detective, constantly searching for clues and collecting data points from well-designed experiments that yield insight as to what's working and what's not with a healthy dose of skepticism for holistic model results.

While the book outlines the importance of great ad performance, it also highlights the courageous use of judgment and risk taking in marketing decisions. Data analysis can reduce risk and uncertainty but not eliminate it, and the best marketers forge ahead.

We live in an era when advertising, especially video advertising, is far different from the "interrupt and watch" model of TV's glory days. That model is long gone, and the challenges for advertisers are changing—the advertiser must figure out how to connect with empowered and fickle viewers who now have the ability to skip or avoid ads altogether. So the measurement of ad quality needs to adjust as well—it is no longer sufficient to just measure viewers' reactions once they've viewed the entire ad. No brand or agency can assume that an ad will be viewed at all. Marketers' priorities have changed from "how do I make an impactful ad?" to "how do I get my ad viewed in the first place then still make it impactful?" How do we get viewers to make that split-second decision not to skip the ad?

Creative teams focus on creating ads that cause a viewer to make that choice to pay attention and "stop and watch." They are even aspiring to go beyond "stop and watch" ads to create "seek and share" ads—ads that viewers choose to not only view but also to actively participate with and share with others, becoming advocates for it.

All of these objectives have metrics to evaluate relative success. Ultimately, it's important we understand what works when it comes to ads, and we can do that by experimenting. From there, we can improve the experience and performance to benefit all of the ecosystem participants—advertisers, creators, publishers, and most importantly, the viewer.

This book leverages the Ace Metrix database, but it is not intended to be a science textbook. It's designed for creative teams, brand teams, chief marketing officers (CMOs), and other constituents who have a stake in ad campaign success. I hope brand marketers and industry people will find this book informative, innovative, and entertaining. It is intended as a guide for all those who are anxious to push the creative envelope.

SECTION ONE

OPTIMIZING CREATIVE: THE SCIENCE OF ART

If you cannot measure it, you cannot improve it.

—Lord Kelvin

Chapter 1

CREATIVELY CHALLENGED?

*Advertising people who ignore research are as dangerous
as generals who ignore decodes of enemy signals.*
—David Ogilvy

In the mid-1980s, I used to say, "If advertising were scored like baseball, we would only count the pitches." At the time, we were working on some of the first marketing-mix analyses that quantified the effectiveness of various elements in a marketer's toolbox: TV advertising, print, trade and consumer promotions, and so on. Our work at that time still applies to much of the analysis of marketing effectiveness today. Before these models and the access to fast, granular data, the industry wasn't equipped to measure advertising effectiveness based on a viewer behavior—the "hits or runs." Rather, the industry was primarily focused on measuring how many ads were delivered and to whom—the pitches. It is a tonnage business in which the quality of the ad itself took a back seat to how many eyeballs were reached, at least for TV anyway. Over time, the models have improved somewhat, but the industry still buys and sells based on "how many" not "how good." More elaborate "performance" metrics have surfaced for digital, but beyond paying for clicks or some other form of engagement, most video ads are still bought and sold on a cost-per-thousand impression (CPM) basis: how many people and what types of people are going to see it—the impression itself is viewed as a commodity.

Yet everyone in the industry realizes that not all ads are created equal. We all know, even through our own personal viewing experience, that a wide variety of good and bad ads air every day. Some ads have the ability to connect emotionally with viewers—to inspire, to influence their behavior. Some are downright dreadful, causing viewers to dive for the remote control to change the channel or immediately skip or leave a website. Even more dangerous are the ads that fail to attract any attention at all but become wallpaper in the viewer's mind. To be ignored is the worst advertising outcome.

I have spent my career fascinated by why some ads achieve greatness while others fall flat. I have been interested in measuring viewer reaction to quantify these differences and to uncover markers that indicate the reasons—the measurement science behind the art.

Ace Metrix is a technology/research company that focuses on quantifying the elements that make video advertising creative successful. It provides a clean read of creative breakthrough power, disentangled from in-market influences, such as media weight, share of voice, program scheduling, contextual synergy, and so on. It identifies and isolates how and why the ad works.

Advertising is of interest to everyone. For one thing, it's unavoidable. We are all bombarded with ads fighting for our attention. Some studies show that the average consumer is subject to over 20,000 ad impressions of all sorts per day when packaging, labels, static outdoor ads, and so on are included. Nielsen says the average US viewer watches over one hour of TV commercials per day or 13.25 minutes of commercials per viewing hour. We love them, we hate them, we sometimes pay attention to them even though we don't want to, and they influence our behavior.

Our research shows that about 10 percent of the US viewing population is "ad-adverse"—people who will do almost anything to avoid seeing ads—a number that is smaller than you might think. But most of us fall somewhere in between the range of barely tolerating them to mildly enjoying them to actively engaging with them. It all depends on the product being advertised and how effective the creative is for the individual. Most of us have something to say about advertising and what we think about a certain ad, whether we liked it or couldn't stand it. So, even if you are not in the advertising field, keep reading this book. You will get to understand what brands are trying to do and whether they're successful. You might find some of the tactics and strategies they use to grab your attention truly fascinating.

The reason there's so much money flowing into this industry (estimated to be at some $70 billion for US TV alone in 2015) is because ads actually do work. So while some people may not like them, ultimately, we're all drawn to them. It's a part of our pop culture, and people can't help but have an opinion about them.

US TV* vs. Digital Video** Ad Spending, 2012-2018
$ billions and % change

	2012	2013	2014	2015	2016	2017	2018
TV*	$64.54	$66.35	$68.54	$70.59	$73.77	$75.98	$78.64
% change	6.4%	2.8%	3.3%	3.0%	4.5%	3.0%	3.5%
Digital video**	$2.89	$4.20	$5.96	$7.77	$9.45	$11.12	$12.71
% change	44.5%	45.3%	41.9%	30.4%	21.7%	17.6%	14.3%

Source: eMarketer, June 2014
*Note: includes broadcast TV (network, syndication & spot) & cable TV; **data through 2013 is derived from IAB/PWC data; includes advertising that appears on desktop and laptop computers as well as mobile phones and tablets; includes in-banner, in-stream (such as pre-roll and overlays) and in-text (ads delivered when users mouse over relevant words).*

Figure 1: According to eMarketer's forecast through 2018, ad spending for digital video is growing at a rapid rate, however, TV ad spending also continues to grow and maintains the largest portion of the ad spend pie.

TV continues to have the largest dollar share of the advertising pie, and contrary to many Silicon Valley "experts," it is still healthy and growing. Ads continue to pay for the production of quality content in TV broadcast programming. Many people outside the industry are unaware of just how expensive quality content is these days, and we all know that amateur content usually is no substitute. TV viewing continues to grow, and premium content on digital isn't free. While new distribution models are surfacing, such as Hulu and Netflix, the fundamental truth is that ad dollars, especially from the up-and-coming, high-quality, high-CPM video ads, will continue to fund the production of new program content, if not exclusively, with subscription models also contributing. The lines will blur, but the largest screen in the house will continue to draw viewers, wherever the content is sourced from.

Of course, digital video is growing by leaps and bounds, which is increasingly becoming device agnostic. Mobile video is also emerging as a new channel, and both are growing faster than any other part of the advertising ecosystem. The point here is that full-motion, high-quality video advertising is growing on whatever screen it is viewed. Video just allows advertisers to tell their story more precisely, convey information, create brand identity, and connect emotionally with viewers more than any other advertising medium.

In the last few years, the industry has improved its ability to deliver high-quality video experiences to any screen. In fact, research companies, which originally focused on measuring only television ads, now often partner with digital players like Facebook, Twitter, Google, and many brand advertisers who have jumped into the digital video pool.

Clearly, digital advertising continues to grow and shift from static or rich media banners to video. A recent report, the Jefferies *Top 10 Themes for 2015*, directly calls out video and programmatic as the top two: "Online video will continue to be the fastest-growing segment in digital advertising. 'Programmatic direct' becomes an increasingly important way to buy digital advertising."

Digital video is still projected to be about 10 percent of the size of TV advertising, but it is growing fast (30 percent in 2015, according to eMarketer). Yet it's also important to note that most brands use repurposed TV ads when running digital video ads. Today, over 90 percent of branded video content online are repurposed TV spots. There is less "web/mobile only" content than one might think.

Brands are finally embracing digital for three key reasons. The first is the potential targeting and measurement benefits, which, despite some growing pains, are superior to those of any other medium. The second reason is the emergence of digital video at the scale and quality needed to effectively tell the brand story, and finally, the ability to buy and deliver the advertising in an automated fashion (programmatic).

Despite the growth of and attention to video ads across all platforms, the focus of innovation in ad tech has been primarily on ad delivery: targeting and tracking systems, timing and context, and performance optimization. Very precise systems were developed to identify "who" the ad should be delivered to, but very little time or innovation was focused on measuring the *"with what"*—what ad should I actually show them or how good that ad is in the first place. Even with the best targeting and measurement, a bad ad, even if it is well targeted is still just a bad ad.

But how can we systematically measure the effectiveness of ads prior to airing? How do you tell whether an ad will be successful or not? What do you compare it to? How can you make it better? Because, according to a Reinartz and Saffert study, "product and brand managers—and the agencies pitching to them—have lacked a systematic way to assess the effectiveness of their ads, creative advertising has been a crapshoot." Our mission is to solve this problem.

As I like to say, "Researchers would often rather be 'right' than 'useful.'" The fact is that with all of this ad technology innovation, the market research industry simply did not keep up. Research companies tried to differentiate themselves through obscure and irrelevant math differences, yet collected, processed, and presented the data the same way that was done generations earlier. The result was that while traditional copy testing (or pretesting) to evaluate the effectiveness of creative still exists, it was far too expensive, slow, and limited in competitive reference to impact the decisions marketers are trying to make. In short, the marketing technology evolution that created the need for faster, better answers had left the old-school researchers in the dust. Companies that chose to think differently have emerged and prospered because of this gap. It's time to avoid the autopsy of a campaign and leverage technology to face current marketing challenges as they are occurring.

The industry had always known that creative matters. But until recently, there was no scientific way of evaluating how effective *every* creative is and the interrelationships between brand messaging that hits viewers simultaneously. When creative was debated, it was often an emotional conversation with hard data being scarce. The key is to provide the data input to impact the creative decision—measuring not where or whom the ad goes to but the *with what*: how effective the ad unit is that's being delivered.

You, the viewer, will respond to a particular ad based on four factors:

1) The quality and reaction to the creative itself

2) Your opinion and experience of the brand prior to viewing the ad

3) Your opinion and experience of competitive brands

4) The external microeconomic and macroeconomic environmental factors

All four of these factors will affect your perception of an ad. This makes creative evaluation even at the individual level a challenge, let alone combining effects of exposure, competitive campaigns, seasonal effects, etc.

There isn't a lot brand marketers can do about factors three and four, but they still need to be factored into a discussion about creative objectives. Brands need to understand what they are up against.

The best of the best brands table below shows the top advertised brands that aired at least 50 unique ads over the past five years. These brands illustrate incredible skill in connecting with viewers consistently over a variety of campaigns and messages. Using metrics that will be discussed in more detail later, these brands' creative scores were consistently higher than competitors ads within their respective categories.

Top 20 Brands, Gap to Category Norm, 2010-2014

Rank	Brand	Brand Norm	Category	Category Norm	Gap to Norm
1.	Google	586	Websites	500	17%
2.	Best Buy	556	Other Stores	510	9%
3.	Walgreens	553	Other Stores	510	8%
4.	Visa	545	Credit Cards	510	7%
5.	Pizza Hut	601	QSR	568	6%
6.	Bing.com	529	Websites	500	6%
7.	Weight Watchers	507	Health & Fitness	481	5%
8.	Olive Garden	622	Restaurants	590	5%
9.	Petsmart	536	Other Stores	510	5%
10.	Budweiser	509	Beer	486	5%
11.	Southwest	574	Airlines	548	5%
12.	Hershey's	591	Candy & Gum	565	5%
13.	Coca-Cola	574	Soda	551	4%
14.	Dairy Queen Other QSR	591	QSR	568	4%
15.	Victoria's Secret	531	Other Stores	510	4%
16.	Ford	545	Non-Luxury Auto	525	4%
17.	Ubisoft Video Games - Family	554	Video Games	534	4%
18.	Domino's Pizza	589	QSR	568	4%
19.	Jeep	544	Non-Luxury Auto	525	4%
20.	Apple iPhones	593	Mobile Devices	572	4%

Figure 2 represents the top 20 brands with the highest percentage gap to respective category norm. Gap-to-norm percentage is based on each brand's average Ace Score for all ads to debut between 2010 and 2014 (minimum 50 ads).

Congratulations to these outstanding marketers! It's one thing to produce one great ad, but it's quite another to produce great work, year after year, campaign after campaign. Compared to other brands in their category, these brands have consistently outperformed them.

It's important for marketers and agencies to have a common, syndicated assessment of creative quality, allowing all players to have a conversation about creative success, with a common denominator of real consumer feedback. Together with the expertise of all players—creative teams, account execs at the agencies, brand teams, even networks—teams can make smarter ad and media decisions, not working from opinions about the creative effectiveness but with data-based truth. There is a lot of ego involved in the creative process, and data helps keep them grounded.

We all know, from our own viewing experience, the difference between a great ad and a horrible ad. It's still surprising to me that, even today, you see TV ads that make you wonder how they got through the creative approval process, because they're just so bad. Yet despite what seems obvious to viewers, it is actually a difficult thing to measure creative success consistently, at scale, and across industries and creative objectives.

And it can be an expensive, potentially career-ending mistake. A TV campaign in the United States can cost $70 million to $100 million or more. In 2015, running an ad during the Super Bowl, which is at the apex of expense, costs $140,000–$150,000 per second. *Per second.* We will spend some time reviewing recent Super Bowl advertising later in the book, but the point here is that the media is very expensive, largely undifferentiated, and represents a huge investment and risk for the advertiser. A brand will typically spend about 90 percent of its ad budget or more on buying the media and less than ten percent on producing the creative asset itself.

There are dozens of industry studies, the American Association of Advertising Agencies (4As), the Association of National Advertisers (ANA), the American Marketing Association (AMA), the Advertising Research Foundation (ARF), that all generally agree that two-thirds or more of the effectiveness of the campaign, or two-thirds of the ROI of that campaign, can be directly attributed to the quality of the creative. *Two-thirds* of the impact for only *10 percent* of the cost!

Great Creative Matters and Provides Leverage

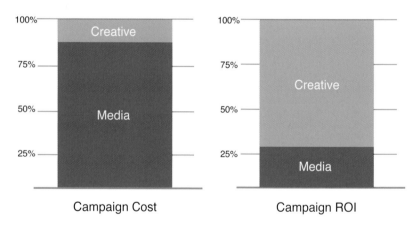

Figure 3: Media is significant but marginally differentiated. Creative is the smallest portion of campaign cost yet has the greatest ability to impact ROI.

Creative leverage is when there is a large improvement in an ad campaign's performance through relatively small creative investment.

Similar studies come to the same conclusion. According to a recent Cox Media publication, "Investing in Quality: The Importance of Creative Advertising Content," creative is the single most important factor in the impact of advertising, accounting for 52 percent of the ad's effect over time. A *Harvard Business Review* publication, "Creativity in Advertising" by Werner Reinartz and Peter Saffert, found that money invested in highly creative ad campaigns had nearly double the sales impact of money invested in less creative ad campaigns. In addition, the study went on to show that "diverting money from the airtime (media) budget to creative will result in a more effective campaign. In fact, the model shows that the company could cut airtime spending by over half a million dollars before the negative impact of reduced airtime outweighed the positive effect of creativity."

The research is undeniable that if your creative is brilliant, you're going to have tremendous leverage in making that campaign successful in delivering the brand objectives and, ultimately, selling more product. Further, we know that millennials *expect* ads to be creative. More than other demographic groups, they "want to see *entertaining* advertising that captures their *attention* and speaks to their *conscious*" according to the recent Cox Media study. The question is how you can know and be sure it's brilliant? How can it be measured consistently? Marketers need to adopt a "test and learn" culture. Test all of the executions thoroughly, in context, and compare it to every other ad out there, and build your own database of experience of what works. Too often, current marketing practice has a haphazard approach to creative measurement—a CYA checkbox without really exploring how and why the creative works with viewers and how it is differentiated. Or brands lump creative assessment in with other campaign evaluative tools. This results in a muddled view of the simultaneous effects of creative, multiple executions, media weight, and other in-market effects, making it almost impossible to accurately measure. Brand and creative teams need a pure read into the creative effect on a viewer, not a rough proxy; they need to act like the future of the brand is at stake with every ad that touches their consumers, because in many ways, it is. That single ad will either improve or degrade the viewer's relationship with the brand in measurable ways.

Today we live with the converging forces of traditional TV, with its high, immediate reach and potential emotive storytelling, and digital, with its highly precise targeting and measurement. We know the market is big, and the stakes for ad creative failure are extremely high. We also know that some of the existing tools are insufficient to reduce the risk. An approach to measuring creative systematically is a needed input, something that provides real-time creative performance insight for every ad airing. Fundamentally, advertising is about competing for human attention, which is increasingly difficult to obtain. Yet great creative has a way of being able to grab and keep human attention, break through, inform, connect, and inspire passion. Measuring creative is the science of the art.

Chapter 2

AVOIDING THE CAMPAIGN AUTOPSY

Never stop testing, and your advertising
will never stop improving.
—David Ogilvy

Beyond just measuring ad quality quickly, arming marketers with insight on what action to take to improve before executional spending occurs is key. Insight comes by understanding your brand's ad in context with other ads that are also being delivered to your consumer. Without context, you are just looking at yourself, acting like your ad is the only ad running, when, of course, it is on a battleground, fighting for viewer's attention. The best ads will win. So, testing each ad creative in a pure way (without confounding market influences) and having the ability to compare it to every other relevant ad gives marketers the best shot at a successful campaign.

About 5,800 to 6,200 ads air nationally every week in the United States, and around 10 percent of those are new. Ace Metrix measures virtually every new ad, closest to debut, providing unique comparability of data. You only know how good your ad is, if you know how good every ad is—context is everything in understanding ad quality.

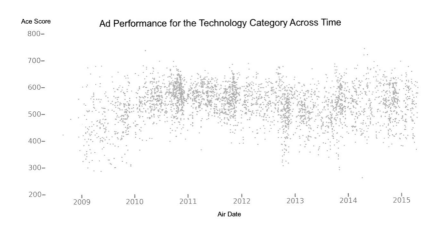

Figure 4: This image illustrates ads within a single category over five years where each dot represents one ad.

Traditional research practices caused problems with advertisers. According to brand marketers and CMOs, production timelines were so tight once budget was approved, many clients had to launch an ad campaign prior to receiving their copy test results. There simply was not enough time given the budget, production schedules, and slow test turnaround. And if the ad proved to be ineffective, there would be millions of dollars' worth of media that would have to be either substituted or pulled, or the subpar ad was just allowed to run with lackluster results.

It was time to disrupt that whole process and beg the question, "What if you could test five versions of an ad and get the results back tomorrow? And what if you could tweak them again and add a different logo treatment or slightly different voice-over or different music or other changes and rapidly test and get the results of making those changes?" Now you have a process in which creative development becomes *iterative*, fueled by real data in which marketers can participate in the process. Our philosophy is to integrate real-time consumer signals within the creative process so that by the time the ad is out of development and into final film, it is perfect. Many creative agencies now swear by using iterative creative data to inform the creative process—not to judge it but to optimize it. It's a collaborative process now, not interfering with the creative ideas but fostering them with data-based viewer insights along the way. Not only do brands save time but they also improve the creative output while mitigating the risk. That's what we set out to do—perfect a process to ensure great creative execution emerges from it. Speed of data and normative context are critical to achieve this. Ace Metrix is not the only solution but a useful one when focusing on the evaluation of the creative itself.

Chapter 3

THE SIMPLICITY OF A SINGLE SCORE

Simplicity is the ultimate sophistication.
—Leonardo Da Vinci

The Ace Score® was developed to solve an age-old industry problem of measuring ad creative: How can I understand the impact of my own ad as compared with all of the other ads that are running against it. The Ace Score is one approach to measure how successful the creative is, not how creative the ad is. It is a single number score that is applied for every ad that airs, to provide marketers with context and simplicity, yet also provide underlying details of why the ad performed the way it did. The Ace Score is often misinterpreted as evaluating or judging creative effort or talent, visuals, music, or effects. In fact, that is not the case. The Ace Score was designed to diagnose how the ads affect viewers consuming them, not assess pass/

fail rankings. In addition, while the aggregate Ace Score is useful when comparing ads, it's made up of seven key components that reveal more specifically how an ad is received. These components can point to difference between ads because ads have different creative objectives and definitions of success.

Additional scientific metrics have evolved that isolate the advertiser's performance objective, see if that objective was achieved, and more importantly, discover how to optimize improvement. Thus, in addition to the single-number aggregate Ace Score, other diagnostic metrics, such as ad personality profiles and individual component scores can highlight particular characteristics of the ad's impact and emotional connection with the viewer. These additional diagnostics help explain how ads perform differently, even with similar overall scores such as one ad having a high information score while another was high in attention. As important as the quantitative data behind each ad is, qualitative data from viewer verbatim comments inform brand teams on their thoughts and reaction—in their own words— and add human context to the data scores.

BEHIND A SYNDICATED SCORING PLATFORM

Every ad tested within the technology platform is based on 500 representative viewer's answers to nine basic questions. These questions assess the key components of Attention, Likeability, Desire, Relevance, Information, Change, and Watchability. These seven base-level performance markers are rolled up using a proprietary algorithm to produce an aggregate score for the ad: the Ace Score. The Ace Score itself was the brainchild of Dr. Ju Young Lee and Steve Goodman, the original founders of Ad Rating Co., which ultimately became Ace Metrix back in 2007. In addition to quantitative scores, viewers complete one open-ended question to elicit viewers' general comments and two behavior questions (what the viewer liked most about the ad and a question related to their familiarity and usage of the brand represented in the ad). This qualitative data provides a window into the viewers' state of mind.

The Ace Score is on a 0–950 scale reflecting combined performance across seven key dimensions shown to impact ad performance. Ace collects verbatim feedback from viewers and mines these comments using natural-language-processing algorithms to generate scores of emotional sentiment and funniness, among others. While the company continues to add metrics of ad behavior, the Ace Score remains a core, holistic measure that provides comparability across brands and categories over time.

The Ace Score and the component scores have been validated by dozens of brands across many industries. While variables used as success criteria can vary widely by brand and industry, the Ace Score, component scores, and gap-to-norm scores have proven to be successful in driving desired outcomes. One such extreme example appears in the chart below, which represents the relationship between aggregate Ace Scores and performance of the S&P 500 over a three-year period.

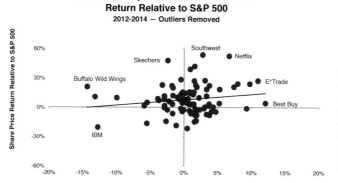

Ace Score Gap-to-Norm vs. Share Price
Return Relative to S&P 500
2012-2014 — Outliers Removed

Figure 5 illustrates the relationship between aggregate Ace Scores and performance of the S&P 500 over a three-year period.

The results above were found using the following methodology:

- Identify all brands with at least five ads in each of the last three years. This yielded 203 unique brands.
- Map these 203 brands to their parent companies. This yielded 144 unique parent companies. Three outlier brands were removed because of abnormal adverse financial condition.
- Calculate annual share price returns for all US-listed parent companies. This yielded 97 annualized return series (2012, 2013, and 2014, and multiyear spans). The other 47 companies were either privately held or were traded on non-US exchanges.
- Test the significance of the relationship between a company's average Ace Score gap-to-category norm to its share price performance relative to the S&P 500, which turns out is significant at the 80 percent CI.

Of course correlation does not necessarily imply causality, but it is interesting that there is a statistically significant positive relationship between Ace Score performance versus category norm and stock market performance. For clients, we can establish relationships between creative performance and their specific KPIs, whether direct sales effect, website visits, showroom traffic, brand favorability etc. For this example I wanted to use the most extreme case where there are so many factors that could impact share price other than ad quality that despite this, there is still a positive relationship. It's most likely that companies that focus on creative quality are likely to do other things well, that together would positively impact overall performance reflected in share price.

Chapter 4

SOME OVERALL LESSONS LEARNED

Creativity may well be the last legal unfair competitive
advantage we can take to run over the competition.
—Dave Trott

The Ace Metrix database includes some 50,000 creative ad tests across 200 categories and thousands of brands—each unique ad having the same methodology with at least 500 geo-demographically balanced respondents. Here are some lessons learned:

1) It's hard to make a great ad.

2) Ace Scores vary a lot by category.

Across all of the ads tested, less than 1 percent score above a 660 Ace Score, and less than 15 percent score above 600. The average Ace Score across the entire database for this five-year period is 533.

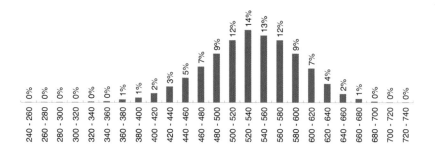

Figure 6 presents the percentage of ads to fall within each 20-point Ace Score range.

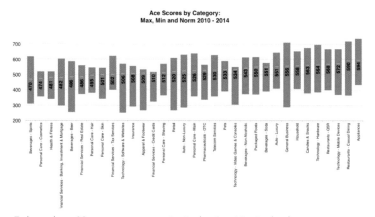

Figure 7 shows how 33 common categories in the Ace Metrix database compare to each other in terms of variability and effectiveness. The chart is organized with the lowest category norm Ace Score on the left and the highest on the right. The high and low ranges of each bar reflect the maximum and minimum Ace Scores within each category for the last five years.

Not surprisingly, there is significant norm variation across product categories and subcategories. An antacid or toe fungus remedy doesn't arouse the senses and emotions as delicious food or a cool, new-featured smartphone or a trip to Hawaii would. This is why comparison with category norms is so important and an integral part of the database. In addition, norms must be current. Some companies have normative data going back decades, which I liken to comparing a smartphone ad to one for Memorex audio tapes. And worse still, these norms are only for one brand, not the entire category. Because the volume of unique ads tested is high, category norms are computed on a rolling 90-day period to reflect the most current competitive market conditions. Norms with long histories have limited use because consumer attitudes to the category vary. For example, automotive and banking ads showed much lower interest during the height of the recession than before and after the recession. Further, the competitive sets in category norms change over time. New restaurant brands, such as Chipotle and Panera Bread, weren't in anyone's competitive view a few years ago.

Providing normative data for ad response is important context for marketers. The ability to customize norms or a brand's competitive set can isolate how an ad might perform against what is most relevant, for example, custom norm definitions for various consumer segments or even types of ads, such as animatics, long-form content video, Facebook autoplay ads, ads with a beach theme, and so on. Changes in category norms year over year show potential creative shifts and also indicate shifts in consumer receptivity to ads in the category. Note, in the table below, that increases in the household, real estate, banking, and credit card categories are reasonable given the improving economy. Video games/consoles declined the most, given the competitive difficulties in that category.

Year over Year Category Ace Score Ranking, 2014 vs 2012

Category	2014 Rank	2012 Rank	Change
Restaurants - Casual Dining	1	2	+1
Appliances	2	1	-1
Household	3	7	+4
Technology - Mobile Devices	4	4	0
Packaged Foods	5	9	+4
Restaurants - QSR	6	6	0
Technology - Hardware	7	5	-2
Beverages - Non Alcoholic	8	12	+4
General Business	9	3	-6
Candies and Snacks	10	8	-2
Auto - Luxury	11	10	-1
Pharmaceuticals - OTC	12	16	+4
Pets	13	14	+1
Personal Care - Main	14	17	+3
Auto - Non-Luxury	15	13	-2
Financial Services - Credit Cards	16	20	+4
Beverages - Soda	17	11	-6
Retail	18	18	0
Telecom Services	19	15	-4
Personal Care - Shaving	20	21	+1
Insurance	21	19	-2
Financial Services - Real Estate	22	33	+11
Health & Fitness	23	27	+4
Personal Care - Skin	24	28	+4
Financial Services - Banking, Investment & Mortgage	25	29	+4
Financial Services - Tax Services	26	23	-3
Beverages - Beer	27	30	+3
Technology - Video Games & Consoles	28	22	-6
Apparel & Footwear	29	25	-4
Technology - Software & Websites	30	24	-6
Personal Care - Hair	31	26	-5
Beverages - Spirits	32	32	0
Personal Care - Cosmetics	33	31	-2

Figure 8 presents the rank position of each category in the Ace Metrix database, based on average Ace Score for all ads to debut in the year represented.

GOOD ADS DON'T WEAR OUT

Across dozens of cases among market-trending products, provided the ad's Ace Score is equal to norm for the category or higher, there is little indication that ads wear out over time. There are very consistent scores, even when ads were tested years apart. Great creative has a lasting impact. As you can see from the examples below, a lot of brilliant creative ads from years ago have just as strong an effect today as they did when they came out.

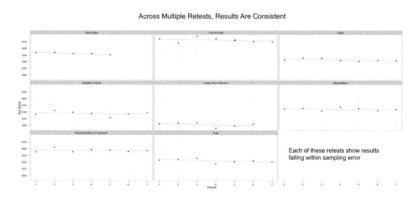

Figure 9: Ace Metrix tested a variety of ads in an internal reliability test, testing the ads over time. Data shows remarkable stability of ad performance over time despite increased frequency.

In this example we are using creative performance over time, with varying frequency. But there are separate studies that show wear out is less than expected even at high frequency levels.

We've learned that great creative ads have a direct impact on the business but are generally rare and difficult to achieve. We also know that when they have been produced, they have staying power with viewers and don't wear out as fast as lower scoring ads.

Chapter 5

THE MANY MEASURES

"Nothing is more efficient than creative advertising. Creative advertising is more memorable, longer lasting, works with less media spending, and builds a fan community…faster."
—Stephan Vogel, Ogilvy and Mather

The Ace Score is a multidimensional, holistic score of creative success reflecting many attributes of an ad's impact on a viewer.

I will briefly describe each component of the above schematic and outline how advertisers would use this data.

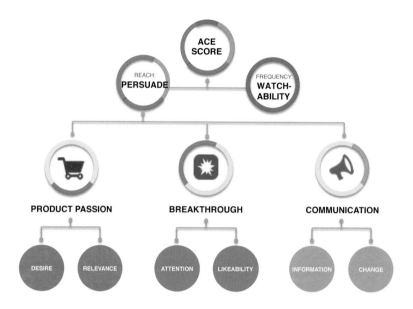

1 ACE SCORE

A holistic view of ad performance across multiple dimensions of effective advertising, a single number that captures the relative ability of an ad to both immediately persuade and enhance memory by inspiring repeat viewings

3 KEY DIMENSIONS of PERSUASION

"Persuasion" is itself a composite score that embodies 3 key dimensions of effective advertising: 1) product passion; 2) the creative's ability to break through; and 3) communication

6 PERSUASION LEVERS

Each dimension of persuasion is further deconstructed to enable a powerfully nuanced view of the breadth & depth of ad effectiveness

Figure 10 represents the various quantitative components of the Ace Score.

Breakthrough is measured by a combination
of Attention and Likeability.

ATTENTION

One of the most important dimensions is whether or not the ad captures a viewer's attention. Attention and Likeability form the breakthrough performance dimension of an ad. Breakthrough ads will be discussed later. High Attention scores are usually but not always a good thing. For example, Volkswagen ran an ad a couple of years ago in which a man woke up in a happy home environment, kissed his wife and kids, backed out of his driveway—and was crashed into. It was a shocking situation, and it scored high on Attention, although it scored average-to-low on Likeability and other dimensions. If shock value and grabbing attention was part of the objective, the ad certainly succeeded. Another example was an ad from a pest control company that created creepy-looking bugs crawling around a kitchen table. The spot scored very high on Attention but far below the norm on Likeability and other metrics.

LIKEABILITY

Likeability is simply measuring viewers' response to whether they liked the ad or not. It is a key driver of ad breakthrough in conjunction with Attention. Viewers can like an ad for many reasons, so Likeability is often used in conjunction with verbatim comments and an additional question that addresses consumers' favorite thing about an ad. In addition, high-impact, viral ads score high on these two breakthrough components: Attention and Likeability.

Product passion ads are powered by Desire and Relevance.

DESIRE

"I want that" is a measure of purchase interest/intent. We sometimes see ads that are likeable and tell a great story, but if the product is not relevant to viewers, ads score low on these dimensions. An example would be that of someone who does not drink beer but who enjoys the Budweiser Clydesdale ad. For a non-beer drinker, that ad might score high on Likeability but low on Desire or purchase intent. Since sales are the ultimate performance measure, understanding desire creation is important for most ad executions.

RELEVANCE

Relevance simply means the ad is relevant to the viewer, and this is obviously important. Relevance can be high or low depending on product familiarity or usage and separates effects such as Likeability from a real purchase intention. For example, a viewer might find an ad for Pampers that features young children as "likeable," but if they don't have diaper-age children, the ad is not relevant to them.

In addition to desire and relevance, there is a question to help diagnose viewers' current product usage and brand perception to further clarify their state of mind when viewing the ad. Product familiarity, as we will discuss later, is the biggest driver in a viewer's perception of an ad.

Communication is powered by
Information and Change metrics.

The communication dimension of the Ace Score is comprised of Information and Change component scores. These are often considered the most rational part of the advertising equation—how an ad communicates specific information or generates an "I didn't know that" response from a viewer.

INFORMATION

This simply measures the degree to which the viewer learned something. Some automotive ads with high Information on torque and MPG score highly on this component, whereas highly emotional story-telling ads may convey little, if any, new information.

CHANGE

This means the company is moving in a new direction and often indicates new, innovative products or features, when used with other scores. Change also registers higher when new or surprising creative is used.

The six component scores above formulate the Persuasion score.

WATCHABILITY

The last element making up the Ace Score is Watchability (or re-watchability), which is a measure of a viewer's willingness to view the ad again. This is useful for media planning purposes as well as for gauging the ad's optimal length. For ads that run relatively long, such as some long-form digital videos (such as the Dove Sketches ad that ran three minutes), many viewers score the ad highly on other dimensions but lower on Watchability because, although they liked it or were moved by it, they are unwilling to make the time investment again. Still, some ads that have gone viral on social media score high on Watchability—some humorous ads people would watch over and over again.

The Persuasion component score is combined with the Watchability component score to form the Ace Score.

In addition to the Ace Score and its underlying components, there are several other separate diagnostic scores also computed for each ad.

BRAND ID

This is the measure that shows a respondent's ability to identify the brand that was advertised in an unaided brand question. Brand ID is expressed in a word list or word cloud. A recent Toyota Avalon example is shown below. In this case, brand recognition was very high, with 88 percent of respondents citing "Toyota." These scores are useful when compared to prior norms for the brand, as well as compared to other brands in the category.

Figure 11: The Brand ID indicates the percentage of respondents to correctly identify the brand advertised. In this example, the Toyota brand and the Avalon model were recalled highly by viewers.

FUNNINESS

Using data mined from viewer verbatim comments using Natural Language Processing algorithms, Ace Metrix computes a "Funniness" score by picking up specific words such as *laugh, funny, humorous, hysterical, LOL,* and so on. Approximately 20 percent of all ads have a humorous objective. The measure is reported as a percentile versus all ads. It is interesting to note that there is an almost zero correlation between how funny an ad is and how effective it is. In fact, there are several examples of ads that are funny but score poorly on effectiveness measures. These can be ads that feature a funny gag or situation but don't communicate information, or they may offend people, or people cannot identify the brand being advertised.

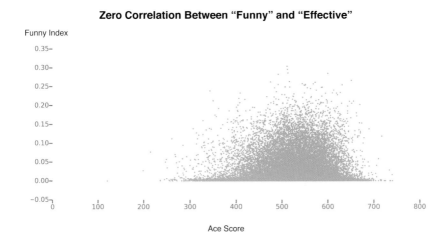

Figure 12 demonstrates the zero correlation between "funny" (the funny index) and "effective" (Ace Score).

High Funny Score, Low Ace Score

Brand	Ad Title	Funny	Ace Score	Length	Air Date
Keystone Light	Woman Doesn't Eat Red Meat	97	395	0:30	4/9/2011
State Street	Grown & Still Holding the TV Antenna	87	378	0:30	8/27/2012
Miller High Life	Rob Talks About Football	91	378	0:30	3/8/2011
Ally	Man Sings In The Shower	91	377	0:30	5/16/2011
Breckenridge	Gravity	95	375	0:15	5/10/2011
Southern Comfort	Beach	90	373	0:30	7/24/2012
Boost	Singletary's Ready/McMahon's Ready	89	372	0:30	1/26/2010
Southern Comfort	Karate	91	370	0:60	9/2/2013
Ad Council	The Talk	90	368	0:30	10/18/2013
DISH Network	Fun Arts	93	368	0:30	9/30/2013
Nissan	Two	90	368	0:45	11/17/2012
Bud Light	Vampires	88	367	0:30	8/31/2010
Gillette Shaving	Mayne: Good Segment	90	365	0:30	6/10/2010
Hornitos	Purer Than Your Intentions	86	360	0:15	4/21/2011
Target	The Roommate And Her Gathering	86	355	0:15	7/13/2010
Geico	Super Heroes Talk Saving Money	86	351	0:30	10/16/2010
Geico	Geico Commercials Are Usually Funny	91	349	0:30	12/1/2010
RadioShack	Man Pours PDA Out Of Cereal Box	86	349	0:15	6/7/2010
Nationwide Auto Insurance	WGS: Discount Finder	89	346	0:30	2/15/2010
Old Navy	(www) Supar Tool	91	336	0:60	6/7/2011

Figure 13 represents the ads with high "Funny" scores and low Ace Scores, based on ads to debut between 2010–2014.

Note that the ads in the above example scored very high on "funny" but low on the Ace Score. Typically, these ads are either specifically targeted to a specific demographic that finds them funny but that others may find distasteful, or they could score low because there is not a clear relationship between the brand advertised, the message, and the funny situation. These ads would be best utilized online to avoid wasting media dollars that don't appeal to a large mass market.

High Funny Score, High Ace Score

Brand	Ad Title	Funny	Ace Score	Length	Air Date
Liberty Mutual	Beautifully Imperfect World	100	670	0:60	7/29/2012
M&M's	Wife Wants Snack	100	656	0:30	6/14/2010
Kohler	The Contractor	99	669	0:30	9/12/2011
Doritos	(SB 11) Pug Attack	99	662	0:30	2/6/2011
Doritos	(SB 12) Slingbaby	99	671	0:30	2/5/2012
BMW	Vet	98	597	0:30	8/15/2012
Snickers	Jeff Turns Into A Diva	98	663	0:30	2/15/2010
Heinz	Hum :15	98	659	0:15	3/20/2014
BMW	(AUG) Vet	97	668	0:30	8/15/2012
M&M's	(SB 12) Just My Shell	97	671	0:30	2/5/2012
Twix	Boss Tells Employee to Get Out	97	659	0:15	7/28/2014
Klondike	They Meet Each Other.	97	665	0:30	4/14/2014
Snickers	Focus Group	97	668	0:30	1/11/2011

Figure 14 represents the ads with high Funny scores and high Ace Scores, based on ads to debut between 2010–2014. Note: Ad titles that include "(SB …)" indicates an ad that broke during a Super Bowl. Ad titles with an "(AUG)" indicates an ad that was scored against an augmented, high income sample.

The above chart shows some of the best examples of high-scoring funny and highly successful ads. These ads were funny across demographics while still delivering on Ace Score components, particularly driven by Likeability and Attention. Several of these ads appeared during a Super Bowl and achieved high breakthrough (Likeability and Attention scores) with audiences.

EMOTIONAL SENTIMENT

Using the same approach with NLP, words associated with positive or negative sentiment are used to compute a score. Ads such as the P&G ads for moms that aired during the Olympics scored very highly on Emotion, for example. As seen in the graph below, Ace Score and Emotional Sentiment show a stronger correlation but still not high at .11. This means that while there is some relationship between a positive emotional dimension and overall effectiveness, it is not a guaranteed driver of success. I read this the other day: "Pamper yourself. The right touch to turn your day around. Whether you're stuck in a rough patch, feeling under the weather, or just in some need of some extra kindness and care, 'this product' will pamper you with indulgence that lifts your spirits and inspires a smile." Clearly, the brand is trying to establish an emotional connection with the consumer. Can you guess what product it is? Facial tissue. I think they might have overshot the runway a bit. Sometimes, consumers just don't want an emotional relationship with a product, but regardless, emotional connection of the ad can be measured.

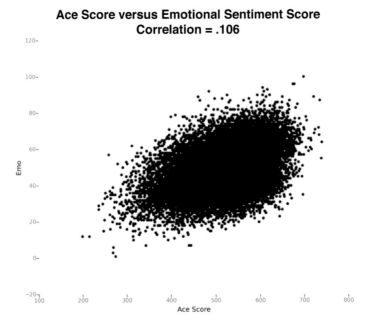

Figure 15 shows the correlation between an ad's effectiveness (Ace Score) and its ability to connect emotionally (Emotional Sentiment score), based on approximately 40,000 ads.

There is a small correlation between how emotional an ad is and its overall effectiveness score. But interestingly, there are many examples where emotion and Ace Score move in different directions as shown in the above plot. This can occur when the brand over-reaches on the emotional attempt but is disconnected from the consumer's perception of the brand.

High Emotion, High Ace Score

Brand	Ad Title	Emo	Ace Score	Length	Air Date
Hyundai Luxury Auto	(AUG) (SB 14) Dad's Sixth Sense	76	706	0:30	2/2/2014
Dawn	Dawn Saves The Wildlife	100	699	0:30	4/7/2010
Ore-Ida	Fresh Take On Ore Ida :30	77	689	0:30	1/20/2014
Samsung Large Appliances	Designed With Everyone In Mind	85	685	0:30	5/24/2010
Hyundai Luxury Auto	(AUG) (SB 14) Dad's Sixth Sense	67	681	0:30	2/2/2014
Budweiser	(SB 14) Puppy Love	83	681	0:60	2/2/2014
Dawn	Mother Can't Protect From Oil	96	675	0:30	6/27/2011
Friendly's Restaurant	Consolation Prize	76	669	0:30	7/21/2014
Atlantis Resort	(AUG) Summer Fun	82	666	0:30	6/8/2014
Residence Inn	A Room To Spread Out And More	85	663	0:30	3/30/2012
Coca-Cola	Try Again	76	662	0:30	11/15/2013
Tide	Any Drum Size Or Temperature	80	661	0:30	2/25/2012
Mercedes-Benz	(AUG) (SB 13) Soul	77	660	0:60	2/3/2013
Kohler	Sometimes You Just Need To Flip	76	657	0:30	8/7/2010
McCormick	Waiting Is Worth It	77	657	0:30	11/10/2014
Mr. Clean	He Looks up to His Grandmother	78	655	0:30	7/7/2014
Craftsman	Fly Through	78	655	0:60	11/9/2014
Cheerios	Heart Healthy Diet	79	654	0:30	4/28/2014
Lowe's	A Fresh New Start	80	652	0:30	4/2/2012
Mercedes-Benz	(AUG) Triumphant	89	651	0:30	5/29/2010

Figure 16 represents examples of ads with both high Ace Scores and high Emotional Sentiment scores.

The chart above shows examples of ads that had high emotion scores and also generated high effectiveness scores (and could also generate a high funny score). In many cases, ads that feature animals typically generate high emotion scores. Some of these ads were Super Bowl ads such as the Budweiser "Puppy Love" and Hyundai's "Dad's Sixth Sense." These are excellent examples of where the emotional connections did align with the brand

High Emotion, Low Ace Score

Brand	Ad Title	Emo	Ace Score	Length	Air Date
Lexus	(AUG) No Overnight Success	71	517	0:30	2/6/2012
Lunchables	Boy Makes Sound Like Sea Lion	71	515	0:30	4/5/2010
Hebrew National	Kid :15	71	515	0:15	6/20/2011
Kashi Cereals	Smile Guarantee	81	514	0:30	2/28/2011
Lexus	(AUG) Your Present	74	513	0:30	11/18/2011
Best Western	Stay Twice & Get A Free Night	71	512	0:30	6/14/2010
Pampers	Happy Dry Babies	71	511	0:30	8/27/2012
Lexus	(AUG) No Overnight Success	71	509	0:30	2/6/2012
Pampers	Vertical Chair Climb	70	502	0:30	4/9/2012
Ciroc	Honoring The Red White And Blue	72	492	0:30	7/8/2011
Cool Whip	Get The Love	74	492	0:15	6/14/2010
Volvo	(AUG) Beautifully Inviting Inside And Out	72	492	0:30	7/18/2011
Pampers	A Baby Plays By His Own Rules	71	489	0:30	7/16/2011
General Mills Cereals	Three Rainbow Marshmallows	70	487	0:30	7/1/2013
Lexus	Make It Count	73	476	0:30	9/3/2012

Figure 17 represents examples of ads with high Emotional Sentiment scores and low Ace Scores. Note: Ad titles that include "(AUG)" indicate ads that were scored against an augmented, high-income sample.

Above are some examples of ads that generated high emotion but did not perform well overall (garnering low Ace Scores). Note that while ads in this list have a strong emotional appeal, that alone does not make the ad successful. Many of these ads include an emotional dimension such as family or babies but lack some other dimension such as relevance, connection to the brand advertised, etc. Or, the ad's length might be a factor, particularly with longer ads that fail to keep the viewer's attention, or with shorter ads that fail to effectively communicate the message.

Some of the highest emotion ads we have tested are from P&G's mom's campaign during the 2012 Olympics as well as their "Dawn Saves the Wildlife" ad, which first debuted days after the Gulf of Mexico oil disaster and shows rescue workers cleaning the oil off of birds.

As I mentioned earlier, we measure how successful the ad creative is compared to norms across all demographics, not how creative the ad is. This is an important distinction for the artists out there. A recent Subway "Two for $2" ad could be very successful in driving the business, although one could question whether it was truly "creative." Clearly, this was a promotional ad identifying an attractive offer. The ad scored well with a 670 Ace Score. It is in the top quintile and scores significantly higher than the category norm of 570. It is not the most visual or creative ad per se but is very successful in communicating the offer, appealing to food consumers and, in fact, driving sales. The ad scores high on information, change, relevance, and desire. Food-oriented ads often show this product passion personality—which we will discuss later—rather than a breakthrough personality. Many would say this ad wasn't creative, although it did have "sell." But it's important to give these types of ads credit where credit is due because they are successful in achieving the brand's objectives. There are many paths to greatness when it comes to advertising, reminding us of David Ogilvy's words, "If it doesn't sell, it isn't creative."

However, if a brand or agency is interested in what viewers liked best about the ad, that is captured in the "Best Thing" question. A high percentage of viewers thought "the visual scenes" were the attributes they like best about the recent ads listed below. These ads' visuals are indeed stunning.

Ads with Large Percentage of Respondents Indicating "Visuals" as the Best Thing

Brand	Ad Title	% Select "Visuals"	Length	Air Date
Lexus	(AUG) Strobe Jumping	53%	0:30	7/14/2014
Lexus	Strobe Jumping	49%	0:30	7/14/2014
Volvo	(AUG) We Are Volvo	47%	0:30	4/14/2014
Invesco	(AUG) Conquer Convention :60	45%	0:60	8/30/2014
Volcom	Thrill Seeker	45%	0:30	6/7/2014
Hawaiian Airlines	Picnic	45%	0:30	9/2/2014
Bass Pro Shop	Gear For Adventure	45%	0:30	3/24/2014
Adidas Men's Footwear	Raptor :60	44%	0:60	8/6/2014
Canon	Hollywood Caliber	43%	0:30	5/23/2014
GE Corporate Branding	(AUG) Thrillingly Predictable	43%	0:30	10/5/2014

Figure 18 depicts examples of high scoring ads in which consumers identified the visuals as the best thing about the ad. Note: Ad titles with an "(AUG)" indicates ads that were scored against an augmented, high-income sample.

This question allows viewers to select the "single best thing about the ad" from a list of options, such as characters, music, visuals, etc. This example shows the ads with the highest proportion of viewers selecting "visuals" as their single best thing.

The measures build off the belief of marketing guru David Aacker that "functional benefits are not the sweet spot of persuasion and communication. Rather, what grabs people are emotional, self-expressive and social benefits." By being able to isolate these emotional effects with hard data, marketers are able to deliver the promise of creating emotional and successful ads.

Chapter 6

AD PERSONALITIES AND PERSONAS

There isn't any significant difference between the various brands of whiskey, or cigarettes or beer. They are all about the same. And so are the cake mixes and the detergents, and the margarines... The manufacturer who dedicates his advertising to building the most sharply defined personality for his brand will get the largest share of the market at the highest profit.

—David Ogilvy

In today's highly cluttered media environment, where consumers are increasingly inclined and technologically enabled to avoid ads, the key challenge advertisers face is how to get people to pay attention, stop and watch, and emotionally connect so strongly with a brand that they are inspired to seek and share ads. The need to be paid attention to and the need to emotionally connect are not unique to advertising. They are fundamental to the human condition. As such, it follows that powerful creative development and media execution can come from looking at video advertising through the humanized lens of ad personality to work with a combination of human characters, voices, and situations. Is your ad more of a "performer/entertainer" born to stand out in a crowded room and grab attention, or is it more of a "professor" whose ability to educate will shine brightest after attention has been achieved but who may struggle to get students to show up to class? Is your ad a "converter," a change agent that is actively reshaping brand imagery? Does it have a persona that might cause you to duck into a store and hide if you saw it coming toward you down the street, or does it have more of a "re-engager" persona that might inspire you to actively reach out and say, "Hello. Nice to see you again"? We all have grown comfortable with how to deal with the diversity of human personality types in our daily lives, so it's not surprising that increased clarity can come from better connecting our wealth of life experience to the maybe-not-quite-so-unique chal-lenges of creating stop-and-watch and emotionally powerful seek-and-share advertising.

The Ace Score is a powerful measure of holistic ad quality, and as such, will always remain the centerpiece for quickly sorting through our massive and continually expanding database of industry-wide ad performance.

However, it is very clear that the objectives of many ads are, by design, *not* holistic in nature (particularly true for viral ads). We appreciate the diversity of ad strategies and therefore have developed a similarly diversified approach to ad assessment. As we like to say, great creative advertising can come from many different creative objec-tives. Some ads are designed to capture attention, some create strong emotional connections, others inform about products, features, and benefits, some are intended to immediately drive sales, and so on. Different metrics are required to measure campaigns appropriately, depending on what they are trying to do.

One of the new uses of the Ace Score data is the combination of scores that lead to visual ad personalities. The ad personality framework allows us to group the Ace Score components and look at the relative difference between them, for each respondent. Likeability and Attention form the breakthrough dimension. Desire and Relevance form the product passion personality, and Information and Change form the communication personality. As you will see, each ad will display its own personality across these dimensions. While the overall Ace Score is a measure of the breadth of an ad's appeal across a variety of dimensions, personalities are a purer way to look at specific ad objectives.

In the graphic on the next page, both Ad One and Ad Two had high Ace Scores. Ad One was for a quick service restaurant (QSR) that showed delicious food and an attractive offer. This ad operated at a somewhat Pavlovian level, appealing to the basic human impulse of hunger. Most of the ads that show delicious food score well and have similar personalities, pulling higher in dimensions of Desire (viewers want the advertised food) and Relevance (most people like food). However, this particular ad also communicated information generating higher overall scores than norm. The ad on the right was a Budweiser ad from a recent Super Bowl. It starred a puppy. Who doesn't like puppies? Apparently, almost no one. The ad scored well but very differently from the restaurant ad. Performer ads, such as this one, quickly jump from the crowd; they were born to break through the clutter and get people to take notice.

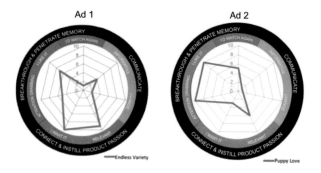

Figure 19

Ad Three is for an Xbox Kinect Sports video game. This ad also scored well and, in fact, was part of the campaign that earned Xbox the title of Brand of the Year in the Video Games/Consoles category for 2014. But this ad personality looks very different from the other examples. It is highly informational and product-feature focused, and the personality is informative, different, and high on desire ("I want one!"). This is also an ad that people would choose to watch again.

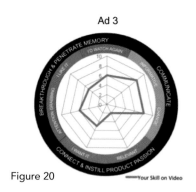

Figure 20

Ad four is for Magic Eraser, a new Mr. Clean product. The ad scored very well, but this is not a breakthrough ad. Many people said it did not hold their attention, but it communicated many of the key products of the household cleaner. The personality is character-ized by information, relevance (most people clean), and a viewer attitude of "I want it." But these types of ads

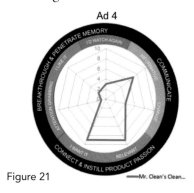

Figure 21

are "re-enforcer" ads that inspire us through desire and relevancy, generally because of a pre-established interest in what they are selling.

Ad 5

Figure 22

The final example is Google's "Search On," end-of-year 2014 ad, an excellent piece of creative work that shows a year in review by featuring the most-searched elements throughout the year. Brilliantly done, this ad scored very well, was high-breakthrough, and grabbed and held attention. Everyone liked it. It was highly relevant to everyone, but it was a long ad, which led to lower re-watchability scores.

These personality visualizations, along with the overall Ace Scores, yield unparalleled clarity about how the ads work.

Why measure so many variables and emotional impact? Renowned marketing expert David Aaaker said it best: "Too often, brand strategists suffer from what I call the "product-attribute fixation trap" whereby there is a compulsion to focus on attributes under the faulty assumption that people are rational... A brand is more than its attributes and functional benefits. It has emotional benefits, self-expressive benefits, social benefits, a brand personality, organizational associations and more. When you understand that, your potential for creating deeper brand experiences and stronger brand/customer relationship will be realized."

The ad personality framework is extremely useful when relating to the specific advertising objective. We know from our data that viewers with a positive perception of the product being advertised, familiar with, and using the product, tend to score the ad much higher than viewers who are unfamiliar or dislike the product. Product passion ads, focusing on Desire and Relevance scores, work well with campaigns focused on existing users or people with a positive predisposition to the brand. But these ads may not work well with non-users. To reach these consumers, brands often use more breakthrough-oriented ads to grab attention and start the conversation. Or brands can try to appeal at a more rational level, creating high information ads to highlight a competitive difference.

Chapter 7

CREATIVE CONSIDERATIONS FOR DIGITAL VIDEO

TV content is not going anywhere; it's going everywhere.
—Serge Matta, CEO, comScore

DIGITAL VIDEO IS NOT THE SAME AS OTHER DIGITAL ADS

From a creative perspective, digital display (banner ads) is not the same as video—duh!

While this sounds obvious, display ads (static banner ads on a webpage) and digital video are often evaluated the same way in some programmatic buying platforms. Behaviorally, viewers respond very differently to a video versus a banner ad. On average, research shows that viewers spend less than one second consuming a banner ad. Some may spend even less than that because they know where the banner ad is on the page, and they have trained their eyes to avoid looking at it completely. It's a phenomenon called ad blindness. We saw that when I worked at Yahoo! with eye-tracking studies that tracked where people were looking. Some people knew where the impression was, so they trained their eyes to move around it on the page and avoided it altogether.

Because viewers spend so little attention to a banner ad, it became clear that the criteria driving performance of banner ads included

- Size of the banner ad
- Relevance of the product
- Viewability of the ad

Size is obvious. Is the ad a whole page takeover or a small border unit? Size will affect whether the display ad gets noticed.

The relevance of the ad to whoever is looking at it is also a key criterion for attention. If the viewers have diaper-age children and they see a Pampers ad, they are going to give it more of a look than people who don't have children that age. That is a decision that is made in half a second.

Finally, many display ads are served but never seen, including ads that are "below the fold" and out of view. Obviously, an ad doesn't have an impact if it isn't seen (see the section on fraud).

However, it's a different experience with video, especially high-production-quality video, which is the reason that brand marketers are flocking to it. The viewer is going to consume online video for an average of 16 seconds (compared with less than a second for a banner). Performance and creative quality is driven by a completely different set of factors than those used for display ads. They are core attributes, such as emotion, funniness, attention, likability, relevance, and so on. These factors are what people pay attention to in a video ad. It connects them emotionally and influences their behavior.

The costs and risks are also much higher for video. The production cost and cost per impression (CPM) to run the video are much higher than for display ads, so brands need to think twice before they run any old creative.

There is a cost for running poor creative: a cost for advertisers (poor performance), for viewers (terrible experience), and for publishers (losing visitors). A number of the top publishers have revealed that there is a significant problem today with the quality of creative that runs in their inventory. Without having a creative standard in place to identify high-quality ads from poor ones, every ad is priced the same. Publishers such as Forbes or Yahoo! come up to me to say, "We can't believe what is running on our networks and are really shocked at the quality of the ad." The bad ads chase site visitors away.

A systematic approach to measuring ad quality that can be accessed by publishers, advertisers, and demand-side platforms (DSPs) to ensure that the quality of the creative is high enough to match a publisher's premium inventory is inevitable. As a result, publishers will demand higher standards in the quality of ad creatives or will charge advertisers more to run poor ads—a penalty tax for poor creative. Creative scoring can guarantee that only quality ads run on publishers' sites.

AND DIGITAL VIDEO IS NOT THE SAME AS TV

The future of advertising is in video because video can tell the brand's story, communicate better, and connect better emotionally with viewers than any other form of advertising. It just works better than banner ads or static billboards. Having a consistent cross-platform creative scoring technology is essential to testing and perfecting digital video ads.

Digital video used to run predominantly on YouTube. But today, according to comScore, 75 percent of all video ads online run outside YouTube.

Digital advertising is filled with the promise of precise targeting, contextual relevance, and emerging, content-based ads, among other things. TV has limited targeting but still wins on immediate reach. You can put it on *The Voice* and get 40 million people to see your ad in a minute. It's almost impossible to get that kind of reach with an online publisher, for example, without it taking a month to build.

But, since national TV is a very fairly blunt targeting instrument, you can only make targeting adjustments around the margins. For the most part, a brand has to assume that the ad is going to reach everybody, more or less. Women watch football, and men watch the cooking channel, and TV is the only device often viewed by more than one person in a household. There is just not that much difference between 18–49-year-olds vs. a 25–54-year-old group. So the best part of TV is immediacy of reach and the ability to pound the message out to millions of people very quickly. The downside, of course, is the lack of precise targeting.

Marketers often test their ads against a particular demographic but forget that a broad TV audience includes all demographics. At least, don't make an ad that offends part of that huge viewing audience. A common mistake advertisers make is to assume that *only* their target viewers pay attention to their ad on TV. As I will discuss in the section on marketing pitfalls, advertising your beer brand with bikini-clad women in a sexist ad on TV might not be the smartest idea in the world since a lot of women will see it—and a lot of women buy beer.

Advertisers sometimes confuse the two media channels and apparently miss that point (i.e., running TV ad campaigns directed at highly targeted segments or high-reach campaigns on specific websites.

A good example is all the pharmaceutical companies who are trying to reach a very small percentage of the population with ads for COPD or Crohn's disease drugs, for example, yet still advertising on national TV, often in primetime, when they even advertise products targeted to younger viewers. We have all cringed when an erectile dysfunction ad airs in a family-viewing environment. Obviously, with over 99 percent of the impressions wasted, these brands still believe it's cheaper to reach that 1 percent by buying TV advertising time, and that may be true. Perhaps, that's the only way they can find their target. But have they taken into account the negative reaction of the 99 percent? Conventional wisdom puts forth that for most products, the more mass market the target is, the better the case for TV as part of the media plan, especially if there is something that is time sensitive, such as a retail sales event when you can't wait for reach to accumulate. The more targeted the market is for your brand, the more you should allocate for digital.

The lines are blurring somewhat as high-reach digital ad networks offer highly targeted reach and TV networks offer some enhanced, "smart" targeting options.

DO PEOPLE VIEW VIDEO ADS THE SAME ACROSS PLATFORMS?

While video on any screen is the future of advertising, the broadcast TV model isn't disappearing any time soon. A marketer's decision to leverage broadcast, cable, online, and mobile is a question of reaching consumers efficiently. The creative quality is generally independent of the modality delivering the ad, and the creative measurement should be as well. This is a key point and something heavily researched at Disney's ad lab in Austin, Texas. In a study presented a couple of years ago that analyzed over 30,000 ads based on screen size, there was no significant difference in the effectiveness or response to ad creative across different size screens. "The smaller screen can be just as effective as the 50-inch display in your living room, because smaller screens are held closer to the eyes and are more interactive. There's an orienting effect where the viewer becomes oriented to that device screen size whereas conventional wisdom would have said video advertising on those small screens can't be as effective, in fact, they can be," said Artie Bulgrin, senior VP of research and analytics for ESPN in a report on the study.

This confirms our own research findings that viewers who see ads on screens of different sizes score the ads very similarly, as long as the details, such as text, were legible on the smaller screens. A more recent study by Yu Me and IPG Media Lab found that video ads consumed on smartphones actually captured a higher attention rate than ads on PCs or tablets. So mobile video is at least as good as other video modalities, if not better, at capturing viewer attention.

TV EVERYWHERE

The multiscreen world of program content consumption has blurred the lines between TV, digital, and mobile as well as between content and ads. People are just as likely to consume their TV content on a digital device or watch time-shifted through a DVR. It seems that TV content has become available on any device, meaning that TV programming content is consumed, time-shifted, on any screen. And it comes with the added benefit of the ability to avoid ads.

According to a report, Alan Wurtzel, president of research and media development for NBC Universal, in the past year, the volume of DVR playback viewing that occurs during primetime hours has reached the point where the DVR now ranks as the number-one network. The ratings generated by viewers opting to watch time-shifted programs from across the TV dial are equivalent to the averages of the Big Four networks combined, according to the NBC study.

comScore released a similar study showing that 34 percent of the time spent by 18–34-year-olds in viewing TV content is done on a desktop computer, smartphone, or tablet, a proportion that is growing rapidly across demographics. "This behavior is no longer about a bunch of 25-year-olds who wear black and live in Williamsburg," Wurtzel said. "It affects everybody across the country."

There is no question that there is a growing amount of TV content being viewed on alternative devices. The key reason, according to comScore, is convenience. Networks are able to provide quick turn-around of popular shows to consumers through restricted-access sites like Hulu and deliver unskippable ads with high CPM's much in line with the traditional TV ad model. High demand TV content can still command a strong ad supported model.

Conversely, sites like Netflix provide delayed and somewhat more limited access to TV content but are an ad-free, subscription model—two opposing models operating in the same ecosystem. There may be some premium subscription models emerging that allow for ad-free viewing of premium TV content, but these have been historically a tough sell to consumers.

Even when programs are watched on the household TV, an increasing amount of viewed content is time-shifted or viewed as video-on-demand. Wurtzel estimated that the viewer size of the streaming component for a show such as *Parks and Recreation* is 37 percent of the total audience, not an insignificant percentage of viewers. According to Nielsen, in 2008, 83 percent of program viewing was done live, and 15 percent was done within three days of a program's premiere. Five years later, live viewing dropped to 60 percent while the other groups skyrocketed.

Of course, as digital continues to grow, a "reach" argument can be made for Internet giants such as Facebook, Google, and Yahoo! reaching hundreds of millions of people every month. But the reach accumulates more gradually than it does with linear TV.

So in a world where consumers are not watching when the broadcast networks want them to and can avoid the ads altogether, how can advertising work? For the first time, the effectiveness of an ad campaign is based on how a brand gets viewers to pay attention to the ad in the first place. No longer can measurement systems be solely based on the impact of an ad, the post-exposure measurement. As stated by Leo Burnett, "If you don't get noticed, you don't have anything. You just have to be noticed, but the art is in getting noticed naturally, without screaming or without tricks." Getting noticed is becoming harder to accomplish, which all cycles back to the importance of brilliant creative. Great content is the only way to ensure viewers will choose to pay attention, unless forced to view it. As Howard Gossage puts it, "Nobody reads ads. People read what interests them, and sometimes it's an ad."

Chapter 8

FROM FORCED TO WATCH TO CHOOSE TO WATCH

We need to stop interrupting what people are interested in and be what people are interested in.

—Craig Davis

What makes digital creative different from TV is that TV ads are created on the assumption that people will watch the entire ad. (Ads are tested by a "forced exposure" method that forces people to watch the entire ad.) In digital media, however, completed ad views are often a rarity. When viewers are given the choice, ads are routinely skipped (like YouTube), closed, or avoided altogether. The challenge for the marketer is to determine what will get viewers' attention quickly enough to ensure they watch the ad to its end. So-called "unskippable" ad formats have emerged but usually have a strong negative viewer reaction, so publishers are cautious to force views. The exception, of course, is the trade-off where a viewer must watch the ads to have access to the premium content they want to watch, and is otherwise unavailable (think Hulu). Three factors are key in evaluating the creative quality of digital video ads: 1) the quality of the creative (Ace Scores and other metrics) post-exposure plus, 2) the likelihood of viewing to completion (second by second diagnostics), and 3) viral potential (the OMG! Factor™).

Stop-and-watch ads command viewers' attention and override their desire to skip them or switch channels. They are destination ads, meaning viewers *choose* to watch them. A new type of video ad is emerging within YouTube and BuzzFeed, among others. It creates high-quality content that interests people who then choose to watch, it just happens to be an ad. The people who choose to watch are often not a representative slice of the viewing population, as the TV audience is, but rather, people who are very interested in the specific ad content. But who cares? People interested in golf are more likely to watch Nike's three-minute Tiger Woods ad. Niche markets are able to find the content that interests this self-selecting group and also create the likelihood of these people sharing that video with like-minded friends. And the ads score very well amongst the "choose to watch" viewers.

A good example is a series of "stories" created by BuzzFeed for Friskies cat food. These are longer-form stories, called "Dear Kitten," where an older cat explains what a dog is to a kitten. Friskies is shown in the vignette, but the ad is not overtly for Friskies.

From an ad personality perspective, breakthrough ads (ads scoring high on Likeability, Watchability, and Attention) are important and positively correlated to completed view-through rates. These break-through ads are designed to grab attention rather than communicate information or product features, and they commonly use humor or emotion to tell a story.

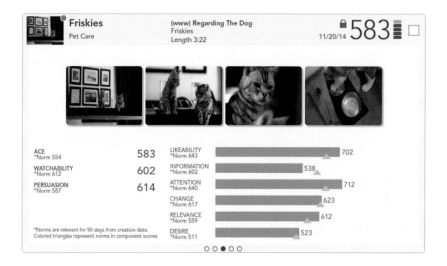

Figure 23 "Regarding the Dog," an ad from Friskies' recent branded content campaign demonstrates strong breakthrough components.

The Friskies long-form ad achieved a whopping 679 Ace Score among cat owners. It displays the breakthrough ad personality, scoring far above norm in Likeability and Attention.

But some of these long-form ads sometimes require different use of scores or different scores altogether to correctly measure the advertisers intent. Many of these long-form ads are more similar to sponsored content that have very little to do with the brand itself. These short films can still be funny and solicit attention but may score low on Watchability because of the length, low on desire (purchase intent), and brand ID. That is appropriate given what the content is trying to achieve and requires the analysis of all the measures, not just one overriding score. The Ace Metrix database allows marketers to compare and benchmark performance of these destination ads versus TV and other long-form ads.

SOCIAL MEDIA AND ACE METRIX EXPERIMENTS

Ace Metrix has worked with many of the world's largest publishers and social media providers on projects that examined the concept that people will take the time to watch great creative ads.

We insisted on ad-testing across a sample of viewers which respresented the entire viewing population, not just visitors or users of a certain site, because viewer reaction is difficult to predict in the real world. It can appeal to people or unintentionally offend people. One member of the social media team told me he didn't like a recent Volvo ad because it promoted a sporty new Volvo, whereas Volvo, in his mind, is best known for station wagons that last forever. My point to him was, "Yeah, but Volvo doesn't want you to think of it as a station wagon company from the 1970s. It wants you to think of it as a new, exciting, upscale brand." So the challenge we had was understanding that the brand's creative objective might be different from a social media user's perception and figuring out how to reconcile the two.

There is a cost to Facebook, Twitter, or any network or publisher for serving a bad ad. And the cost of creating a poor user experience is something these networks care deeply about. Poor performance also costs the advertiser, of course. Nobody wins with terrible creative. This sounds obvious but has never been embraced completely by TV broadcasters. Now, however, the bar is being pushed higher to include not only ads that are good but also ads that have good content that I, the viewer, want to watch.

These Publishers are experimenting with new ad units all the time. One created new "autoplay" premium video ad units that run automatically when a user visits a particular part of a page. The networks are encouraging brands to come up with more impactful creative for these units rather than just reusing a TV ad the brand has already produced.

Part of experimentation is to get creative teams to not simply take what is produced for TV but rather, explore better ways to make these creative units work. Publishers increasingly want to test these ads first to make sure they met creative quality standards and the impact on the user experience was understood.

The result of testing many different versions of the creative? The ad finally became something people would *choose* to watch, improving view-throughs and, therefore, the customer experience. A win-win for all parties.

Interestingly, these social media giants have industry-leading targeting algorithms based on their proprietary identity systems but also have high-reach ad products. In working with Ace Metrix, these brands make sure the high-reach ads do what they are supposed to do. That whole exercise pushed us to realize that everybody who distributes ads and video ads on the web has a stake in improving the quality. Ace Metrix can be the anchor in the measurement system—a key element in measuring and predicting campaign success.

There are several varieties of video ad models out there including ads of various lengths that can be skipped after three, five, eight, and ten seconds. "Unskippable" video formats are also emerging across many platforms. In addition, payments can be made on a CPM basis (e.g., advertisers pay for impression regardless of whether the ad is viewed all the way through) or only on completed views (or some other measure, such as paying for clicks). Regardless of the model, the challenge has shifted to getting viewers to pay attention to the full ad message.

HOW TO GET VIEW-THROUGHS: SECOND-BY-SECOND DIAGNOSTICS

A number of tools exist that can be used to predict a viewer's attention and view-through rates. One diagnostic tool was developed to indicate a viewer's engagement second by second to understand which ads are more likely to be viewed all the way through, based on the first five, eight, and ten seconds. Attention and likeability measurement early in the ad is valuable when you're comparing alternative ads to discover which one actually caught the viewer's attention early, resulting in higher view-through rates. View-throughs are not the only success goal, unless you are an ad network and that is the metric on which you earn revenue. While advertisers and creative teams care about the overall impact of the ad, they need to be mindful of the new reality—that in a skippable ad environment, unless you grab viewer attention early, you are unlikely to have them stick around to the end. Ace Metrix works with many ad networks to predict view-through rates based on creative markers. Ads can often create an experience that builds throughout the ad's narrative and tells a story, but when so many ads are not viewed through to the end, viewers don't see the ad's big finish. It's crucial to incorporate persuasive content early in the ad to help ensure the view will be completed.

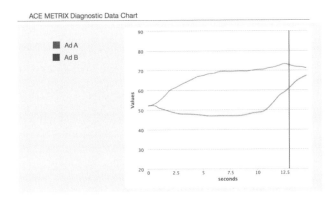

Figure 24

In this example above, the diagnostic trace shows Ad "B" started stronger at the two-to five-second point and generated a 35 percent higher view-through rate because of its fast start, although, at the end, it finished with a lower overall score than Ad "A."

We continue to research this fact that those first five seconds can drive improvements in view-through rate. Starting strong is important when it comes to motivating viewers to watch more of the ad, and we see in our research that ads that exhibit the behavior of Ad B in the above example have been seen to generate 76 percent higher view-through rates than ads that exhibit the behavior of Ad A. This is an important new consideration for creative teams, that although the ad might test the same upon a completed viewing, you might not get to that point if the ad starts slowly. But Ad A scored a 620, while Ad B scored 509 once viewed. For skippable units, media teams should use Ad B, since it started stronger and has a higher probability of being viewed to completion. For unskippable units, Ad A should be selected since its higher score indicates a stronger persuasive impact.

In the example below, we restrict the trace just to males and compare a Clinique ad (Ad A) vs. a pet food ad (Ad B) to illustrate the obvious importance of product affinity on attention, particularly early in the ad. The Clinique ad, not surprisingly, generated low interest and attention for males throughout. These are extreme examples, but understanding what the product is early in the ad is an important contributor to viewing completely.

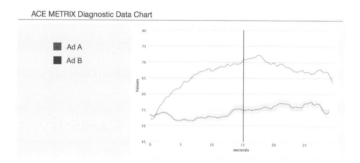

Figure 25

Viewers are more distracted than ever. Think of them as saying, "Impress me within five seconds or else I will skip this ad." To achieve a higher rate of completed views, brands have had some success with the following strategies:

1. ***Be recognizable:*** Something needs to connect with the viewer in the first three to five seconds. (Retread TV ads, for example, are not always successful on a skippable ad unit such as YouTube's TrueView where viewers can skip ads in five seconds.) Typically, data show that brands that can identify themselves early have a better view-through rate among viewers who use and are familiar with the product (product affinity). If I know it's a BMW ad early,

and I have a positive impression of that brand, I am more likely to complete the view.

2. **Create a following:** Ads that have identifiable characters or plot, such as "the most interesting man in the world" or M&M characters, for example, can create view-throughs because of the interest generated by previous ads featuring the same characters (see point no. 5 below).

3. **Foster familiarity:** The data prove that familiarity with a product or ad creates positive emotions and perceptions ("mere-exposure effect"). As with the creation of a following, a series of ads with similar characters or storylines can create this effect.

4. **Script:** As is true of any great 15-second ad, the quality of the script is important in establishing product need and giving the viewer a reason to stick around.

5. **Themes:** It's important to establish ad affinity, not just brand affinity. This can be done by creating ad themes that build on each other and deliver entertainment value or emotive appeal. Some brands "sponsor" entertainment ad content as a means of driving views. For example, they sponsor a comedian for the "joke of the day." Brands with long-standing ad campaign themes, such as the Dos Equis "most interesting man in the world," actually have viewers wanting to watch the next "episode."

6. **Hook:** Be unpredictable: Geico recently ran some unique digital ads where the scene was "frozen" while something else happened. For example, a family was having dinner when they were frozen, and a big dog climbed on their table. This created a curiosity in the viewer and showed

much higher complete rates than other Geico ads because of the absurdity of the situation. The chart below shows how the early viewer response for this ad "Family" trumped other Geico ads. In addition, by creating a surprise effect, viewers will be more likely to view new Geico ads to look for that surprise factor.

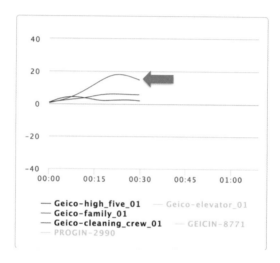

Figure 26

In one Google experiment, a test ad was placed on YouTube and simply displayed a blank screen that said something like "there is nothing going on in this ad." The ad did nothing but generated higher view-throughs than Super Bowl ads, because it a) didn't look like a typical ad and b) the unique message caused viewers to view to understand what it was about.

THE ROLE OF AD CREATIVE IN A PROGRAMMATIC WORLD

We continue to hear a lot of discussion about the "programmatic" media buying and selling systems. It wasn't too long ago when media was bought and sold through a fax machine, going back and forth between a buyer and seller to negotiate the rate, even with digital media purchases. "Programmatic" became an automated way to buy/sell ad impressions through the introduction of ad exchanges, a real-time bidding (RTB) system between buyers and sellers. But programmatic has expanded to be more than RTB; it has automated the entire ad buying and delivery process. According to a leading programmatic player, Rocket Fuel, programmatic will account for 55 percent of all digital (excluding search) ad spend in 2015—over $15 billion.

Programmatic represented a huge step forward with automated ad buying and delivery to specific targets. Unfortunately, it also created a commodity environment for the creative itself, so the most terrible ad was treated exactly the same as the best ad. Measuring creative quality has an important role to play in these programmatic systems.

As shown previously in this book, countless studies have shown that the lion's share of the ROI of a campaign can be directly traced to the quality of the campaign creative. As with everything, quality matters, and this is especially true when it comes to advertising.

The origin of today's programmatic platform was a means to trade remnant (leftover, unsold) inventory at low prices. This worked fine when nobody cared about who the publisher was or the quality of the ad with a low-end impression. But as we move up the food chain and jam higher value/quality impressions, and now video, into the same platform, the lack of quality measurement becomes a big problem. The result is shaping up to be a repeat of the remnant marketplace, putting downward pressure on CPMs, regardless of how good they are. A system in which all ads are treated as equal penalizes great creative.

That will soon change as leading digital publishers, networks, and advertisers move to incorporate video creative quality metrics as part of the workflow to ensure the highest impact ads are given credit and earn the highest quality audiences.

The ad industry is chock full of urban myths and legends. One such myth is that bad ad creatives are not really that bad; no one will notice. But poor quality ads are, in fact, not neutral at all. As previously stated, bad ad experience does lasting and widespread damage to a brand and creates a very vicious cycle.

To make matters worse, cost-per-click (CPC) or cost-per-action (CPA) deals encourage running ads at insane frequency levels and that includes ads with bad creative. That's like playing a song you hate at an unbearable decibel level.

Unlike an exchange, which is a zero sum game with a winner and a loser, improving creative quality floats all boats in the ecosystem.

Ad creative quality measurement creates a role reversal in which brands/agencies with the best work actually "sell" their ad content to publishers in addition to being buyers. To date, the IAB's quality assurance guidelines are all about transparency and fraud protection, a necessary and important priority. But now is the time to really focus on measuring the most impactful measure of quality—the quality of the creative itself.

Publishers can now place a creative quality standard on their most important inventory. For example, if a publisher mandates that only ads that have high Ace Scores or the previously mentioned OMG! Factor are allowed to run, they protect themselves from a bad user experience. Viewers actually are going to choose to watch these high-quality ads and not leave the site. That's what is different about putting a creative quality measurement into these programmatic systems: decommoditizing the creative. Creative drives advertising value, so it is important to coexist and be integrated with programmatic tools.

Chapter 9

CREATIVE AND SOCIAL MEDIA

Social media is the ultimate equalizer. It gives a voice
and a platform to anyone willing to engage.
—Amy Jo Martin, Author

If an ad is going to run on TV, trying it out first on social media can be a smart move. Many social media tools have emerged for marketers to monitor their brand. Even if advertisers are trying to keep the buzz, getting feedback like that can prevent some real disasters. In Super Bowl 2015, for example, 60 percent of ads were put on YouTube prior to the game. But it's also important to remember that while useful, the viewing audience of a particular ad on YouTube might not be representative of the TV viewing audience. By definition, YouTube ads are self-selecting, meaning that only people who already have an interest in the brand or ad are likely to choose to view them.

NEGATIVE ASPECTS OF SOCIAL MEDIA AS A DATA INPUT

One caution to marketers is that just because the social media universe is a large sample doesn't mean it's unbiased. Social media opinions are not representative ones, and researchers and advertisers need to consider the people who have the time or inclination to actually tweet or post based on a TV or other ad. How "normal" are they?

A popular way of looking at social media engagement is the "1-9-90" rule. One percent of people voice the opinion or create the content; 9 percent follow and share; and 90 percent lurk, listen, or ignore. This speaks to how a small fraction of the population can get a big, albeit unrepresentative, voice.

A Jell-O ad experience from a couple of years ago shows how social media can give marketers the wrong signal: Kraft's Jell-O brand was launching a new refrigerated product targeted to moms. They had just hired Crispin Porter, a creative shop known for brilliant and edgy work, to produce a series of ads. The first ad, shown below, had parents in a tongue-in-cheek vignette scare their children because they took

Parents Tell Kids A Story
Jell-O   ACE SCORE: 616

one of their Jell-O desserts. The ad first aired on a Tuesday night, and by Wednesday morning, there was a social media backlash in which 150,000 people liked a Facebook page to boycott the brand for "advocating traumatizing children." Ace Metrix tested the ad and, on the same day it aired, reported to the Kraft team that it had scored well, especially with moms, who thought the ad was hilarious. There were some of the "lunatic fringe" (as I call it) comments in the data, but they came from a very small segment. Kraft had several more ads in production and, based on the data, stuck with the campaign, which turned out to be a huge success. Moral of the story: social media can send signals that don't represent the majority view. The vocal minority expressed an extreme position that was counter to the opinion of the general population.

Another example was a recent Cheerios ad featuring a multiracial family. So many vicious and racial comments were made while the ad was on YouTube that the ad had to be removed. Ace Metrix data showed that most American viewers fully supported the ad, the characters, and the message.

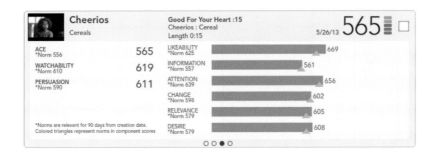

Figure 27

As mentioned previously, viewers' verbatim comments can clarify why the ads score the way they do and how real people feel about the content.

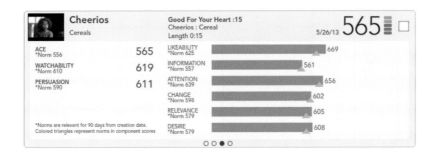

Figure 28

General Mills had the courage to keep running the ad. In fact, the company created a sequel that scored even higher.

Many times, brands overreact to the social media "lunatic fringe" and ignore what their true customer base is saying. Social media can be a damaging and vicious environment where people can spew forth anonymously.

Social media sites attract people who choose to watch ads. The process is highly self-selective. That's not a bad thing, but it's important to note that a high number of views doesn't mean broad reach. In fact, views are not even unduplicated, meaning that if one person viewed the ad 100 times, views are counted as 100, not 1. The Tiger Woods "Did You Learn Anything?" ad in 2010 is a good example. The ad shows him hitting trick golf shots with another golfer. A lot of young male golfers thought the ad was funny and watched it several times. But the data showed that women still viewed Tiger Woods in a negative light after his scandal and, therefore, scored the ad poorly.

Figure 29

It might have been a good idea to put the ad on YouTube first and not run it on national TV until the general public's reactions were better understood. On YouTube, Nike could keep it visible to viewers who would choose to watch it and not be offended.

If you're running an ad on YouTube and you're running an ad on TV, you want to be able to compare the two—or run on YouTube first to assess the impact. Ace Metrix provides an advantage to advertisers by offering a standardized comparison across platforms to determine if an ad is truly ready for prime time.

Figure 30

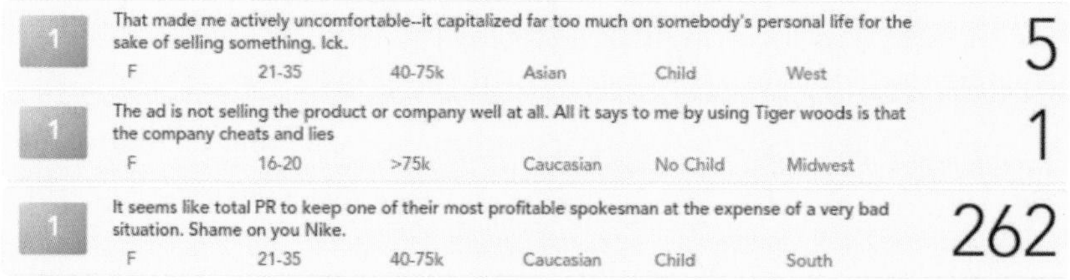

The ad information shown:

That made me actively uncomfortable--it capitalized far too much on somebody's personal life for the sake of selling something. Ick.
F   21-35   40-75k   Asian   Child   West   **5**

The ad is not selling the product or company well at all. All it says to me by using Tiger woods is that the company cheats and lies
F   16-20   >75k   Caucasian   No Child   Midwest   **1**

It seems like total PR to keep one of their most profitable spokesman at the expense of a very bad situation. Shame on you Nike.
F   21-35   40-75k   Caucasian   Child   South   **262**

Figure 31

But if you think you are assessing the overall audience by just testing on YouTube, you might be in for a nasty surprise. In this example, women may be unrepresented because of the self-selection bias—thus the views might indicate the ad is better than it would be for an overall TV audience. It's important to test your ad, and test it against the overall TV viewing audience to get the correct result to determine if an ad is truly ready for prime time.

Finally, the social media data streams can contain very low signal to noise when evaluating specific ad impact. There are many social media listening tools that try to capture social media "buzz" following a TV ad exposure for example. If an ad runs for a casual dining restaurant, then many people monitor Twitter or Facebook in the minutes immediately following that exposure. But the average person doesn't post about a particular TV ad. Most people mentioning the restaurant are saying to their friends "I'm here at the Olive Garden, where are you"—not commenting about an ad.

GOING VIRAL

Understanding what drives viral success is becoming a key component of creative evaluation. "Does this ad have the characteristics of some of the great viral ads of the past?" The OMG! Factor was developed to isolate the key emotional drivers that are consistent with widely shared viral ads. The score doesn't predict whether the ad will become a viral sensation; rather, it indicates the breakthrough components and other elements of the ad that *could* make it a successful shared ad.

Wharton professor Jonah Berger is a leader of viral research. He believes "the relationship between emotion and social transmission is more complex than valence alone. 'Virality' is partially driven by physiological arousal. Content that evokes high-arousal positive (e.g., awe) or negative (e.g., anger or anxiety) emotions is more viral. Content that evokes low-arousal, or deactivating, emotions (e.g., sadness) is less viral."

Verbatim consumer comments contain terms indicative of physiological arousal

Procter & Gamble	(www) Like A Girl				
Corporate Branding	P&G Corp Branding Length 3:20		7/1/14	724	✓

It was the most profound and powerful thing I've ever seen. It made me realize just how insulting 'like a girl\" is when describing actions.I don't know how I never noticed it before. It made me proud to be a girl as I saw the confidence exude from the younger and then older girls. It was a breath of fresh air.

F	21-35	<40k	Caucasian	Child	South

I found this to be a very moving and powerful piece. I felt guilty for all the times I must've used that expression in a derogatory manner. It's so important to empower young women to believe in themselves. This is a GREAT ad.

F	36-49	>75k	Caucasian	No Child	South

Volvo	(AUG) (www) Epic Split				
Luxury Auto	Volvo Length 0:60		11/18/13	633	✓

Okay, while I may not know much about power steering or how it works, this ad absolutely blew me away! I couldn't stop watching it. The music was awesome too - it was so graceful and peaceful. And watching Jean Claude in this ad do those splits while those trucks were moving totally mesmerized me. Love this ad for Volvo dynamic power steering.

F	50+	>75k	Caucasian	Child	Midwest

OMG! That was amazing, classic VanDamme. Wow. Kudos to Volvo, those trucks were amazing. I'm impressed by this commericial.

M	36-49	>75k	AfAm	Child	South

Figure 32

Viral is a whole new aspect of advertising that didn't exist before social media. You could not share a TV ad before social media. Viral ads can be live "experiments" for brands, without the cost and risk of broad TV-based exposure.

Recently, we broke down the viral power of an ad (the OMG! Factor) into three emotional drivers. These are empirically derived NLP scores that comprise what we call the 3 Hs—Humor, Heart, and Hook. "Humor" is the Funny score described earlier. "Heart" is the emotional sentiment score (e.g., inspiring, patriotic, heartwarming, sad, uplifting etc.), and "Hook" is the surprise factor: by use of a clever creative device, the ad grabbed my attention, "hooked me" so that I had to finish it to completion.

Pfizer's Centrum multivitamin brand is a good example of a brand taking a risk and creating a highly sharable ad. Quietly, a couple of years ago, Centrum placed a new ad on YouTube that was radically different from the typical advertising of a fairly conservative drug manufacturer. Think of the typical Centrum ads that are run on TV (see below). The ads have a "product/information" personality. They score well but are more focused on communicating product attributes.

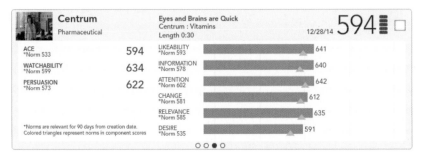

Figure 33: Comparing a typical Centrum television ad to its YouTube run ad.

The "standard" Centrum ad running on TV is powered by Information and Relevance. This is the typical personality of product/information ad creative.

Figure 34: This Centrum television ad "Eyes and Brains are Quick" has a "product/information" personality.

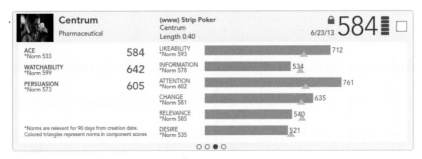

Figure 35

In contrast, consider the ad run on YouTube called "Strip Poker." While both ads scored similarly, they operated in completely different ways. The second ad is a spoof on a "strip poker" game among attractive 20-somethings that turns into a scene at an old-folks home at the end of the ad. It was a hilarious, unexpected take on a vitamin commercial that when put on YouTube, achieved some viral success. Note that the scores for Likeability and Attention were extremely high for this ad compared with Centrum's typical TV ad.

Figure 36: Centrum effectively uses humor in its YouTube ad and achieves viral success.

Now look at the personality of the edgy "strip poker" ad, a wildly different "breakthrough" ad driven by Attention, Likeability, and Change (obviously, this ad is a big change for Pfizer).

This is a good example of how to experiment on digital media without the high cost and risk of a national TV campaign. This edgy ad did have its detractors, so it was probably best to let viewers seek it out. Testing allows brands to determine the best distribution channel for the ad, to be able to see whether it's going to really fly in the market place or challenge the brand a little bit in the wrong direction.

Figure 37 shows the personality profiles of the two ads.

Shown together, you can tell the marketer had clearly distinct objectives for the ads, which had clearly different effects in the marketplace. If gaining attention and breaking through the clutter were the objectives, the strip poker ad was far superior, as was its OMG! score. But if the brand was concerned about an edgy backlash from core, older users, it would have stuck with the product features/benefits ad for the broad TV market and leave the edgy ad on YouTube.

Another good example is Geico's "Hump Day" ad with the camel. Now, that's an interesting and, above all, noticeable ad. Car insurance has nothing to do with a camel that is dressed up in a business suit and walks around an office, talking to people. Yet that ad was funny and belonged to the fabric of pop culture. We could pick that up from the Likeability and Attention scores that were high relative to the other dimensions. While Geico has multiple creatives running simultaneously, this one managed to get over a million shares on YouTube. Breakthrough and OMG! components are apparent in its extremely high Likeability and Attention scores.

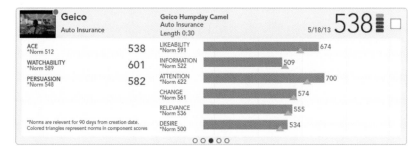

Figure 38

Viral ads can be very effective even when they're not funny. We see that with Dove's "Sketches" ad, which was about three minutes in length and featured a police sketch artist. The theme was women's definition of beauty. The ad was very poignant and became a powerful statement of social attitudes. It aroused a high emotional connection in viewers, and although it was a serious ad, it displayed the same high Likeability and Attention scores of an OMG! viral ad. It is the intense emotional arousal, of some form that drives viral sharing—shock, humor, touching, sad…any emotion that truly connects and is relevant.

Being able to measure viral and emotion triggers allows a brand to predict how likely an ad is to go viral and whether it would be worth paying for additional views to draw more attention to it.

The additional emotional measures now available are leading marketers to gain insight of stop-and-watch and seek-and-share advertising and its viewer impact.

SECTION
TWO

SO WHAT HAVE WE
LEARNED ABOUT ADS?

Chapter 10

ADVERTISING:
HOW PAST ADS LOOK TODAY

"There are a lot of great technicians in advertising. And unfortunately they talk the best game. They know all the rules ... but there's one little rub. They forget that advertising is persuasion, and persuasion is not a science, but an art. Advertising is the art of persuasion."
—William Bernbach

Not long ago I was asked by a reporter to comment on some original, retro ads from the early '40s when TV was just making its presence felt. There were four ads that were all on YouTube. One was for Philip Morris cigarettes, featuring Lucy and Desi Arnaz. One was for Kool-Aid. One was for Coca-Cola, and another was for Brylcreem.

I found it interesting to examine how ads focused on emerging new technologies might differ from old ads. It was instructive to look back at iconic ads from the past and understand how current audiences would perceive them if they were to air again today. Some are timeless and seem as relevant today as they were when they first aired. Recently Gatorade re-aired some famous "Be Like Mike" ads to much success. Others seemed dated or irrelevant. Still others were completely forgotten. Determining why proved to be informative.

What really struck me about the old ads was that the advertisers really focused on the product's attributes, knowing they had a more captive audience than today. They didn't need to try to strive to break through and garner attention. Attention was a given. Back then, the opportunity to skip through the ads or to have a remote control to change the channel did not exist. These ads directly promoted product features and benefits. They also made use of celebrities directly promoting the product ("I use this product. You should too."), which would come across as cheesy and condescending today. Consumers today have a higher level of distrust than they did in the early days of TV when audiences were more naïve. The ads didn't present the kind of storytelling or breakthrough, emotive, beautiful imagery that you see in ads today. They were focused on product delivery and benefits. Communication of product features and attributes is a creative measurement that falls under the Information and Relevance categories in the Ace Metrix scoring system.

Kool-Aid was one such example. In these older ads, advertising was really about creating demand for an aspirational lifestyle. The product and its features were part of that new lifestyle that you, the viewer, could have if you just bought the product. Because advertisers had a captive audience, they didn't focus so much on emotive or more elaborate communication strategies.

Fast forward to today when people aren't captive. They need a reason to watch. Typically, product ads are viewed as boring and are viewed by people who are already interested or use the product. In addition, viewers are more skeptical of the aspirational lifestyle message. They are still used occasionally but have been toned down from the early days.

Throwback Ads: How We Perceive Them Today

The key takeaways from our analysis of old ads are as follows:

- Nostalgia seems to play a strong part in the heightened scores of vintage ads. Participants in a survey are much more likely to score an ad higher if they had seen the ad before the survey, either during the original TV airing or on TV/online after the original airing.
- Across the board, the majority of survey participants think throwback ads are better than current ads.
  - An example of this is Pepsi's "Pepsi Generation" ad, featuring Michael Jackson: 76 percent of consumers say it is better than Pepsi's current ads.
- The majority of survey participants indicate that most classic ads still represent the brand today.
  - This was especially true for Energizer's "Energizer Bunny" ad, with 79 percent of participants saying the classic ad still represents the brand.
- Budweiser's "Bud-Weis-Er" ad featuring frogs is one of the most recognized of ads, with 76 percent of survey

participants remembering seeing the ad when it originally aired.

- Not surprisingly, history-making classic ads often score extremely high in terms of Attention and Likeability when they are tested by today's consumers.

- For nearly every classic ad tested, when participants are asked, "What is the best thing about this ad?" the answer with the highest percentage is most often "the characters." Perhaps, this is a testament to the effectiveness of franchise characters or brand ambassadors.

The following are the test results of classic ads scored by 500+ of today's consumers:

Pepsi's "New Can" (1993)

(TBT) New Can
Pepsi

ACE SCORE: 632

- This ad, which starred Cindy Crawford, was from Super Bowl 37.
- It received an Ace Score of 632, surpassing the Pepsi brand average by 10 percent and the soda category average by 15 percent.
- Sixty-one percent of respondents believe it is better than today's Pepsi ads.
- Fifty-seven percent of respondents think the ad still represents current Pepsi branding "extremely well."
- "New Can" was such a success for Pepsi that it decided to team up with Cindy again. Ten years later, in 2002, Pepsi

recreated the original ad to introduce a new can design for Diet Pepsi.

Cheerios' "Scrooge" (1989)

(TBT) Scrooge
Cheerios
ACE SCORE: 618

- "Scrooge" features Buzzbee and Ebenezer Scrooge and is the longest-running Cheerios ad. Originally debuting in 1989, it still occasionally airs during the holidays.
- It earned an Ace Score of 618, which is 6 percent above the cereal category average.
- Seventy-six percent of viewers believe the brand still represents the ideas and values of the "Scrooge" ad.
- The emotional sentiment score achieved 78 out of 100, which is 28 percent higher than the brand's average.

MetLife's "Peanuts Thanksgiving" (1988)

(TBT) Peanut's Thanksgiving
MetLife Insurance
ACE SCORE: 617

- "Peanuts Thanksgiving" features the lovable Charles Schultz *Peanuts* characters starring in a Thanksgiving play.
- "Peanuts Thanksgiving" received a score of 617.
- The emotional sentiment score for "Peanuts Thanksgiving" was 69, which is 35 percent above the category norm.

- When respondents were asked what they believe is the best part of the ad, 36 percent said the "characters" stood out.
- With an attention score of 724, respondents found the ad appealing, scoring it 15 percent above the 90-day norm for other insurance companies' ads.

Ad Council's "The Crying Indian" (1971)

(TBT) Native American Crying
Keep America Beautiful   ACE SCORE: 704

- Airing in 1971, on Earth Day, the famous ad by Keep America Beautiful and the Ad Council is known for calling attention to the growing issue of pollution and littering in America.
- Forty-six percent of survey respondents indicate that the ad's ability to convey the importance of not littering is the paramount aspect of the spot.
- The component scores for Likeability, Attention, and Relevance are at least 20 percent above the category norm.
- Respondents reinforced the findings, using words such as "message" (10 percent), "remember" (7 percent), "beautiful" (5 percent), and "love" (4 percent) to describe their thoughts and feelings about the ad.

Energizer's "Energizer Bunny" (1989)

- In 1989, the Energizer Bunny arrived on TV screens and "kept going and going" throughout the 1990s.

- The ad received an Ace Score of 662, higher than any other Energizer ad.

(TBT) Energizer Bunny
Energizer   ACE SCORE: 662

- Eighty-four percent of respondents say this ad still represents Energizer's brand values "a lot."
- Of the 368 respondents who left an optional comment, the most common word used to describe the ad was "funny," with 16 percent of respondents using it.

Oscar Mayer's "Bologna Song" (1973)

(TBT) Bologna Song
Oscar Mayer   ACE SCORE: 633

- The jingle designed to teach people to spell *bologna* remains one of the most memorable in advertising history and is the reason why this ad is one of the longest-running ads in TV advertising history.
- The ad scored highest with consumers aged 50+, who awarded the ad with an average Ace Score of 666, which was 11 percent above the meat category norm.
- What is perhaps most significant is that the categories of Likeability and Attention in "Bologna Song" are higher than those of any recent Oscar Mayer ad.
- "Bologna Song" scored 84, which was 56 percent above the meat category norm, 65 percent above the average of all ads in any category, and 71 percent above the Oscar Mayer brand norm.

- Not surprisingly, 79 percent of respondents had seen the ad before, with 59 percent seeing it when it first aired.

Coca-Cola's "Mean Joe Greene" (1979)

(TBT) Mean Joe Green
Coca-Cola
ACE SCORE: 680

- The ad features Steeler's star defensive tackle Mean Joe Greene tossing his shirt to a young fan in the tunnel in appreciation for sharing his Coca-Cola.
- The ad earned an Emotional Sentiment score of 76, which is 46 percent higher than other soda ads and 31 percent higher than other Coke ads over the last year.
- The ad's Ace Score came in at a 680, 20 percent higher than current soda category average.
- Coca-Cola revived the idea in 2009 with modern NFL star Troy Palomalu to launch their new Coke Zero brand (which, incidentally, scored very poorly).
- A different brand, Downy, created "Joe Greene Stinky," a spoof of the "Mean Joe Greene" ad. The ad is universal in that it spawned its own sequels.

Wendy's "Where's the Beef?" (1984)

- The ad earned an Ace Score of 655, one of the highest among QSR (Quick Serve Restaurant) ads, including those tested in the last year.

(TBT) Where's The Beef?
Wendy's   ACE SCORE: 655

- The ad's high score is only partially due to nostalgia, as 32 percent of the survey's 500 respondents had no recollection of seeing the ad before (on TV or online).
- Of the 332 optional verbatim responses, 13 percent use the words "where's" or "beef" when writing a response to the ad.

We remember these ads, some of them decades after they first aired, because they connected emotionally with us at the time and still retain our attention through one of the 3 Hs—Humor, Heart, or Hook. The ads that make us feel a certain way are locked into our memory and achieve the high breakthrough scores of Attention and Likeability. The above example ads were also tightly interwoven with their brand's message, making it nearly impossible to not just remember the ad but also the associated brand and its values.

Chapter 11

WHAT MAKES ADS GREAT?

Rules are what the artist breaks;
the memorable never emerged from a formula. In
advertising, not to be different is virtually suicidal.
—Bill Bernbach

It's really quite simple to describe but difficult to execute. Great ads grab and hold a viewer's attention and communicate the advertiser's message as intended. Be persuasive and watchable, key elements of the Ace Score. But there are many different paths to greatness. Ads can be effective through storytelling, emotion, humor, information, etc.

First off, there is no formula. Getting too prescriptive kills creativity and, by the way, is usually wrong. Ads that break through, inspire product passion, inform the viewer, and influence viewer behavior. Yes, there are many paths to greatness, but two important rules of thumb are 1) determine which vehicle can drive attention and 2) determine the precise message the ad is trying to deliver.

Attention-driving vehicles can include humor, emotion, product-affinity, and so on, giving viewers a reason to stick around.

The key message can be monitored and tested. Viewers can play back what they think the advertiser is trying to communicate, and it is often considerably different from what was intended.

BEWARE OF CELEBRITIES

The Ace Metrix database of 50,000 ads enables a review across a range of ad categories and specific ad treatments. Such a broad spectrum allows us to evaluate whether the use of celebrities helps an ad's performance. In fact, we conducted two separate studies, both showing that celebrities don't help. On average, in a comprehensive study from a couple of years ago and recently updated, ads featuring celebrities performed 3 percent less favorably than ads that don't feature celebrities. The reason is that celebrities almost always polarize—and not just Tiger Woods and Justin Bieber. In any mass-market audience there are many people who won't approve of a brand's celebrity choice. A couple of years ago we studied an interesting cosmetic ad featuring Sarah Jessica Parker. Almost half of the women surveyed loved her and thought she was beautiful; the other half disliked her intensely and did not think she was beautiful at all. Too often, there's no legitimate reason for the celebrity to be featured in the ad in the first place. Marketers need to ask themselves: "What value does the celebrity bring to my brand? Are they endorsers? Do they just look nice or have a pleasant voice? What are they doing here?" For example, Dale Earnhardt, Jr. is selling tax software? There's just no connection. Ads that put the celebrity in the ad to say, "Buy this because I use it" just don't work.

On the other hand, some celebrity ads work very well—recent Intel ads, starring "Sheldon," a nerdy character from *Big Bang Theory*, are a great example. Sheldon sneaks into the Intel lab to look around, a clever high-tech spin that viewers responded positively to. He was playing in character, which viewers could relate to. Remember Betty White in some of the Snickers ads? Snickers wove celebrities in— You're not yourself when you're hungry" or "You're acting like a diva." When the celebrity is woven into the script (as apposed to being the entire focus) in an authentic or clever way as part of the story, the ads do extremely well.

On rare occasions, using a company executive in an ad can work. One of our agency partners had a client whose CEO always wanted to be in the ad. To help them make a solid recommendation, we looked at how effective CEOs are in starring in their own ads. What we found was that CEOs do not make great spokesmen—except in certain cases. One example is Papa John's ad featuring its CEO and founder. Viewers think he's likable and credible. For a CEO to improve the ad, people have to believe the CEO is genuine. The CEO of Domino's was featured in an ad when he relaunched the company in which he said, "It's on me; we're going to do better," and he showed examples of bad things that can happen with poorly designed pizza boxes or poor-quality food. He came across as a buck-stops-with-me kind of person. He was authentic, genuine, and believable; broke through the clutter; and delivered straight talk.

But if a CEO doesn't come across as genuine or his presence in the ad comes across as some kind of gimmick or if the CEO is just boring or not convincing, it ruins the credibility of the CEO and doesn't help the brand. It's a high-risk strategy and mandates testing prior to airing, something that many CEOs have missed in the past.

PUPPIES, BABIES, AND FOOD

So, don't use a celebrity, but *do* use puppies. It's just a fact that Likeability for these elements almost always score above norm with the general public. This formula was adopted by GoDaddy for the 2015 Super Bowl as the company abandoned the racy bikini ads from prior years. However, because the lost puppy was sold using a GoDaddy site, the ad was pulled because of strong viewer backlash. Animals, babies, and food *don't*, generally, polarize. Budweiser's highest-scoring ad of 2014 was "Puppy Love," which was followed in 2015 by another top-scoring puppy ad, "Lost Puppy." The 60-second spot of 2014 achieved an Ace Score of 681, which was 33 percent higher than the 2014 category norm. Most notably, its attention score was 833, the highest such score among all Super Bowl ads dating back to 2010. The 2015 ad scored a 652 but leveraged the same emotion and attention drivers. Especially for broad-reach brands, cute works.

These ads work not because of the characters but because of the story. The story is what carries viewers on a journey, connects with them emotionally, or informs them. But animals and babies are more likely to garner broad attention and likeability than adult characters will.

MATCHING YOUR MEDIA STRATEGY TO THE PERSONALITY OF YOUR AD

The media schedule is important in achieving campaign success. From breakthrough ad data, especially where long ad units are concerned, we see examples of the importance of gaining the highest reach as quickly as possible since the ad, while high-scoring, often is not viewed again. These so-called one-and-done ads score high on Attention and Likeability but are not necessarily chosen to be viewed again. The Watchability score is a good indicator of the likelihood the ad will be viewed over and over. Funny ads often have the ability to break through *and* have high Watchability scores. The Geico "Hump Day" ad with the talking camel, for example, has high Attention, Likeability, and Watchability scores. Quite simply, some ads benefit from repetition; some ads are killed by it—something the media strategy should take into account before running.

Alternatively, KitchenAid created a very high-scoring ad that showed, with beautiful visuals, all the product's attachments as well as food you could create with a KitchenAid mixer. Its strength was not in Attention and Likeability, although these factors also scored high. Its unique drivers were in Information and Change. Strength in the Information and Change scores indicates the ad has more layers for consumers to digest, making it valuable for them to see more than once. The ad conveyed strong product passion personality once viewers' attention was captured. It achieved high product-related scores but relatively lower breakthrough scores. It needed higher frequency than it got to drive home the product benefits. Viewers' attention was more difficult to capture, but once viewers connected, they were more likely to learn about the product and be persuaded to buy.

PHILANTHROPIC MESSAGING WORKS!

Brand ads do particularly well when they support a cause. Wal-Mart and Kohls are just two examples of brands that have run philanthropic ads that score well above their category norms. Wal-Mart ran a campaign supporting the hiring of veterans, while Kohls ran a campaign supporting local schools. Viewers like to know that brands stand for something more than just product features and benefits. It is a consistent theme across the database.

Even if the ads are purely philanthropic but deliver a unique, intelligent message, they typically score above norm. For example, Coca-Cola ran an ad describing the company's response to nutrition complaints. Viewers respected being treated intelligently on an important topic.

MasterCard's "Stand Up to Cancer" campaign, featuring Ray Romano, is an example of one of the highest-scoring ads in the credit card category.

P&G has been able to achieve this connection a couple of times. Dawn launched "Dawn Saves the Wildlife" campaign with its dish-washing soap.

Figure 39

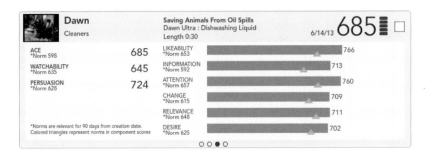

Figure 40

Viewers were surprised by what the brand stood for—how it could help in a crisis. The strong Likeability and Attention scores achieved strong breakthrough.

P&G was also able to achieve this for Tide, which sponsored a campaign of ads showing a big rig truck equipped with washing machines visiting areas struck hard by Hurricane Katrina.

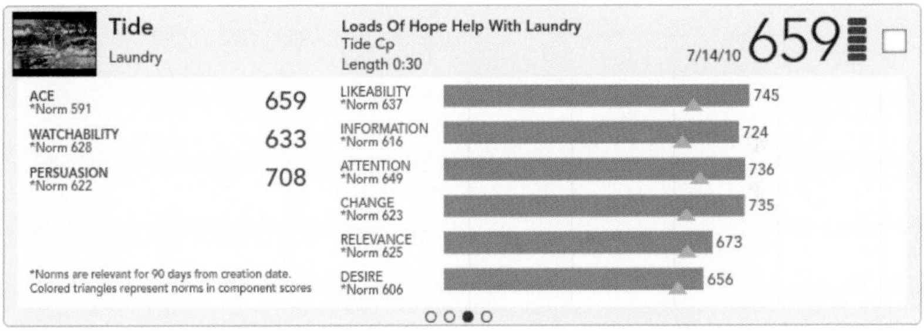

Figure 41

Ads that can get viewers to identify not only with the functional attributes of a brand ("whiter whites") but the brand values ("Tide loads of hope") wind up generating higher scores and being very successful.

It's important to remember that there are many paths to greatness in creative, and ads also have varying objectives. Successful ads are measured in terms of achieving these brand objectives. But, creating successful campaigns is usually about both the idea and the storytelling. Does the ad convey an idea in a way that both connects emotionally with viewers *and* breaks through and compels action?

Chapter 12

SUPER SUPER BOWL ADS

*I am one who believes that one of the greatest
dangers of advertising is not that of misleading
people but that of boring them to death.*

—Leo Burnett

Super Bowl ads represent a unique viewing opportunity for advertisers. It is one of the few times a year when the ads are viewed with anticipation and excitement, almost as much as the game itself. And every year these 50 or so ads help shape the future of advertising.

In terms of audiences, the Super Bowl is the highest-reach event of the year. Viewers in 2015 were anticipated to number over 114 million; one in two households in America tuned in. The game is also unique in that many watch it with a group of other people representing a range of ages.

As a result of the game's huge reach and its prestigious display of the pinnacle of advertising art, Super Bowl ad rates are the highest in history—$4.5 million for 30 seconds or $150,000 per second in 2015.

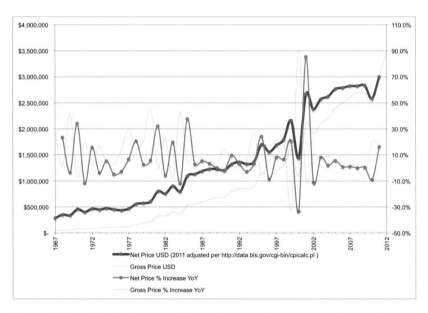

Figure 42: Super Bowl ad rates per 30-second spot and percent growth versus the prior year. Source: "Superbowl 30sec 2011 adjusted" by Dsuchter - Own work. Licensed under CC BY-SA 3.0 via Wikimedia Commons. http://commons.wikimedia.org/wiki/File:Superbowl_30sec_2011_adjusted.png#/media/File:Superbowl_30sec_2011_adjusted.png

Given the career-making or breaking risk, the Super Bowl is no place to wing it. While some Super Bowl ads take calculated risks, it's insanity not to test reactions with audiences ahead of time. Ad strategies used during the Super Bowl vary, but every year we see classic mistakes. As a result, it's important to understand how these ads work, especially since these ads often kick off new trends and are imitated throughout the year.

In 2015, we put together a database of all 315 Super Bowl ads since 2010. While the number of ads represents 0.0007 percent of all ads in the Ace database, they often are the most memorable and successful.

In the 2015 Super Bowl, Budweiser, Coca-Cola, Snickers, Mercedes-Benz, Microsoft, Dodge, and Doritos were among the Top 10 Most Effective Super Bowl Ads. But McDonald's achieved the overall top score with an Ace Score of 706, which is about as common as a perfect game in Major League Baseball. Of all ads aired between 2011 and 2015, only 0.06 percent of them have scored above 700. McDonald's achieved Super Bowl gold, surprising and delighting consumers and changing perceptions about the fast-food giant.

Top 10 Super Bowl 2015 Ads by Ace Score

Rank	Brand	Ad Title	Powered By	Ace Score
1	McDonald's	(SB15) Pay With Lovin'	Likeability, Emotion	706
2	Budweiser	(SB15) Lost Dog	Attention, Likeability, Emotion	652
2	Coca-Cola	(SB15) #MakeItHappy	Likeability, Relevance, Emotion	652
2	Snickers	(SB 15) The Brady Bunch	Likeability, Desire	652
5	Mercedes-Benz	(SB15) Fable	Attention, Likeability, Emotion	649
6	Microsoft	(SB15) Braylon O'Neill	Attention, Likeability, Information, Change	646
7	Dodge	(SB15) Official Dodge Wisdom	Likeability, Emotion	644
8	Doritos	(SB15) When Pigs Fly	Attention, Likeability, Desire	643
9	Always	(SB 15) #LikeAGirl	Likeability	636
10	Doritos	(SB15) Middle Seat	Attention, Likeability	631

Figure 43

In today's highly cluttered media environment where consumers are increasingly inclined and enabled to avoid ads, it's crucial to find ways to get them to stop and watch your ad. Super Bowl ads are under greater scrutiny because the competitive set of ads aired during the game is of a very high caliber. Further, it is well-established that a powerful driver of success is the ability of the ad to emotionally penetrate viewers' hearts and minds. Not only does the McDonald's ad accomplish this in spades, it does it in a surprising way: it taps into the powerful emotions inherent in the durable love of family and friends and implicitly, yet legitimately, connects that emotion with the long-term presence the McDonalds brand has had in our lives and communities—overall, a beautifully executed ad.

Figure 44

The Super Bowl provides advertisers with the largest and most demographically diverse audience available on TV. Here is the list of the top Super Bowl ads over the past five years based on aggregate Ace Score.

Top 20 Highest Scoring Long-Format Super Bowl Ads (60 seconds or longer), 2011-2015

Brand	Ad Title	Ad Length	Ace Score	Year
Microsoft	Empowering	0:60	710	2014
McDonald's	Pay With Lovin'	0:60	706	2015
Budweiser	Puppy Love	0:60	681	2014
Budweiser	Hero's Welcome	0:60	675	2014
Budweiser	Brotherhood	0:60	665	2013
Coca-Cola	The Catch	0:60	654	2012
Budweiser	Lost Dog	0:60	652	2015
Coca-Cola	#MakeItHappy	0:60	652	2015
Mercedes-Benz	Fable	0:60	649	2015
Microsoft	Braylon O'Neill	0:60	646	2015
Dodge	Official Dodge Wisdom	0:60	644	2015
Always	#LikeAGirl	0:60	636	2015
Chrysler	It's Half Time America	2:00	633	2012
Honda	Matthew's Day Off	0:60	630	2012
Pepsi	Kings Court	0:60	628	2012
Mercedes-Benz	Soul	0:60	626	2013
Toyota	Joy Ride	0:60	625	2014
Jeep	This Land Is Your Land	1:30	625	2015
Kia	The Perfect Getaway	0:60	624	2015
Jaguar	Rendezvous	0:60	623	2014

Figure 45

SHIFT TO POSITIVE MESSAGING

For the past few years, we've seen a gradual shift away from sheer shock value and slapstick humor toward positive, emotionally connective Super Bowl ads. McDonald's is on-trend with messages of positivity that really resonate with consumers, and nearly every ad in the 2015 Super Bowl Top 10 embraced this emotional connection, with the exception of Doritos and Snickers, which won on Humor, Attention, Likeability, and Desire.

Positive messaging poses less risk of offending viewers. We have seen the trend away from humorous ads that have the potential to alienate part of the huge viewing audience. It's hard to offend someone with an anti-bullying message or a message about the importance of being a good dad. With all the sentimentality, advertisers also run the risk of being boring or sad at a time when audiences are expecting to be entertained—especially if you watch three or four deep, emotional ads in a row. It will be interesting to see if future Super Bowl crops will go back to more humor and less intense emotion.

In some cases, the "do-good" messaging almost went too far in 2015. In Nationwide's ad, "Boy," viewers expressed shock at the message of avoiding childhood accidents when they realized the boy character died and was not able to enjoy growing up. Some viewers were offended, and many lit up social media with complaints that the ad killed the positive mood of Super Bowl parties. Yet the ad generated some of the highest awareness of any ad at the Super Bowl.

CELEBRITIES: SECRETS OF SUCCESS OR RECIPE FOR DISASTER

As we discussed earlier, celebrities are no guarantee of a successful ad. While celebrities make appearances in one-third of all Super Bowl ads, only one celebrity ad ranked within the top ten highest-scoring Super Bowl ads between 2012 and 2015. In 2014, RadioShack broke this trend by generating a celebrity-laden ad that was the fourth-highest-scoring ad over a five-year period (Ace Score 677). The ad featured not one but a full cast of characters from the '80s to effectively make fun of itself and announce a new launch of the stores. The celebrities in this case—Hulk Hogan, Mary Lou Retton, Alf, Chucky, Cliff from *Cheers,* and a slew of other time-stamped characters—were used to parody themselves rather than to endorse the brand or leverage current celebrity power to earn brand buzz. However, the ad, while well received, did little to change the fortunes of the retail chain, which filed for Chapter 11 bankruptcy protection in 2015.

The pattern continued in 2015. Of the top ten scoring ads, only one ad featured celebrities. This was the Snickers ad spoofing the '70s

Brady Bunch TV series. The Snickers theme of "You're not yourself when you're hungry" has cleverly woven celebrity appearances into the ad storyline for several years. The success of this ad is the strength of the script and use of the characters in a humorous but relevant way.

As we discussed earlier, in the context of general advertising, celebrity ads more typically fall at the bottom of the list. In 2015, Kim Kardashian, one of the most polarizing figures in America, and actor Jeff Bridges, featured in an odd ad for Squarespace, both failed to connect with viewers. In fact, eight of the ten lowest-scoring ads of Super Bowls since 2010 include celebrities (four of the eight are GoDaddy ads, and the rest are by Hulu and the beer brands Bud Light, Michelob, and Stella). When the premium for Super Bowl ad time is so high, why wouldn't brands avoid the celebrity risk or, at a minimum, make sure that their ads are thoroughly tested first? As mentioned earlier, brands need to understand that any celebrity they select will be disliked by a certain number of viewers. Almost every celebrity—even Oprah—has their haters. In addition, celebrities can't carry the whole story. If they are relevant to the script, as they are in Snickers ads, they can be very effective, but just because a celebrity is featured does not make an ad a success.

IT'S ABOUT CUTE, NOT SEXY

Eight of the top ten Super Bowl ads since 2010 have included an adorable kid or a furry mammal, while the ten ads that make up the bottom performers lack either. Broad TV audiences, such as those who watch the Super Bowl, find animals much more appealing than scantily clad men or women in a sex-themed ad. None of the top ten ads (or the top 26, in fact) could be described as "sexy," whereas four of the bottom ten ads attempt to appeal sexually. Overall, the Super Bowl's sexy ads performed 8.3 percent lower than ads without a sexy theme. Budweiser, a perennial user of dogs and horses, scored another top emotional ad with "Lost Puppy" in 2015.

LONGER IS BETTER

While the net cost of airtime during the game has risen significantly year over year, advertisers are increasingly extending their spots to take full advantage of the captive audience. In the 2015 game, 43 percent of the ads ran for 45 seconds or longer compared to 18 percent in 2010 and 20 percent in 2011. When looked at in aggregate, Super Bowl ads earn stronger scores as their duration increases. The average Ace Score rose from 529 for a15-second spot to 572 for a 60-second spot, and ads lasting longer than 60 seconds averaged a score of 580. Why? Because when creative teams have more time, they can create more emotional storytelling using the longer format. In 2014, for example, Microsoft and two Budweiser ads earned top scores for their long-form ads (60 seconds), all three delivering emotionally powerful stories.

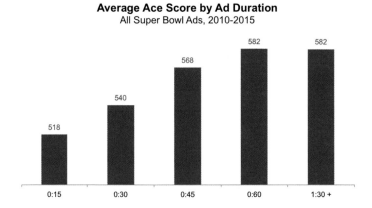

Average Ace Score by Ad Duration
All Super Bowl Ads, 2010-2015

Figure 46

SOCIAL MEDIA INTERACTION

In 2014, advertisers started a trend that continued in 2015. They took heed that isolating one-half of their audience with highly targeted, crass, or otherwise offensive ads is, at best, a waste of money and, at worst, damaging to the brand. In fact, fewer advertisers attempted humor than in previous years. In 2015 less than half (49 percent) were funny as opposed to 64 percent of ads in 2014 and 72 percent in 2013. The funny ads of the Super Bowl scored 563, slightly less than the ads that weren't funny, which scored 573 on average.

In recent years, brands have focused on social engagement to extend viewership of the ad aired during the game to the weeks surrounding the game. Expanding advertising's largest stage beyond whistle-to-whistle is not a new concept. In 2015, we saw some aspects of the social-media-integration plateau. Eleven percent of advertisers in 2015 and 2014 incorporated a blatant use of fan participation in conjunction with their airtime exposure. Bud Light, Carnival Cruises, Doritos, as well as newcomer brands Avocados from Mexico, Dove, and Locktite published their fan strategies prior to game day. This included voting for ads to air, signing up for extended content, or entering a contest. About 50 percent of Super Bowl ads in 2015 were given their own hashtag.

2013 was the year of Super Bowl leaks. Super Bowl 47 marked a significant awakening for advertisers. Gone were the days of advertisers throwing all their eggs into a single Super Bowl basket. Until 2013, brands shrouded their ads in secrecy and sometimes even hid their participation in the Super Bowl until the ads aired on game day. Starting in 2013, however, there was a shift in which 50 percent of all advertising brands issued a teaser ad either online or on TV in the weeks leading up to the game. Forty-six percent actually released their game-day ad early, in stark contrast to prior years, shifting the Super Bowl from a one-ad experience to an extended social media campaign.

Today, Super Bowl advertisers leverage their ad on game day as part of an overall event. In 2015 more than half of the ads were released on social media before the game, and more advertisers released teasers or longer-form versions of the actual game-day content.

THE YEAR OF AMERICAN STORIES

It was at Super Bowl 46 (2012) when more advertisers decided that while 30-second ads were relatively cheaper, 60 seconds or longer was better, and what better time to tell your story than during the Super Bowl? Many of those 60-second ads had a strong patriotic pull, whether a call to arms or tribute. It's here that we saw Clint Eastwood's two-minute ad, "It's Halftime in America"; GE's 45-second ad, "Building Something Big in Louisville"; and Budweiser's ad that harkened back to early post-prohibition nationalism.

While particularly concentrated in 2012, patriotism continues to be a theme used by Super Bowl advertisers. Ads reflecting the American spirit—the value of a farmer in Dodge's Paul Harvey rendition in 2013 (and others) or Budweiser's 2014 salute to veterans, "Hero's Welcome"—capitalize on positive national pride. Automotive floor mat maker WeatherTech appealed to national pride with an ad featuring its use of US suppliers and its employment of US workers.

UNTESTED DUDS

Finally, there are the duds. Every year it seems some brands are content to not test their ads before pushing them out on Super Bowl Sunday—with disastrous results. Many of these offenders have been Internet brands, such as Squarespace, Living Social, Groupon, Hulu, GoldieBlox, and, perennial favorite, GoDaddy. While some of these duds may have been trying to achieve some kind of shock value, the Super Bowl is not the place for such brand risks. In addition, ads such as Jublia's toe fungus treatment in 2015, while certainly driving awareness, fell flat with a Super Bowl audience and scored poorly. Ads for ailments such as toe fungus, incontinence, erectile dysfunction, and even overtly sexual ads typically bomb in a Super Bowl setting with such a massive and diverse audience. People just don't want to see them, at least, not during the Super Bowl and especially in a group setting.

All Super Bowl ads can be seen at acemetrix.com.

SECTION THREE

MEASURING CREATIVE PERFORMANCE

Chapter 13

THE MARKETER'S DILEMMA: TEST IS BETTER THAN GUESS

You can observe a lot just by watching.

—Yogi Berra

Measuring and quantifying marketing performance is a condition of employment for most CMOs today, and the push for accountability will continue. In fact, a recent Duke University survey of CMOs outlined that marketing spending on analytics would increase by 73 percent over the next three years and account for over 12 percent of Total Marketing spending. Data informs all aspects of creative advertising, from concept development, to ad production, to in-market monitoring, to post-campaign analysis. Advertising creative, media execution, and ROI measurement are inextricably linked in today's marketing organizations. In fact, some marketing decisions are dictated by the output of quantitative models. But as marketers constantly try to improve the quality of their work, they need to provide a similar level of discipline in evaluating the quality of their measurement tools and practices, some of which, while well intended, are on shaky ground.

It never ceases to amaze me when companies make magical and mythical claims of precisely measuring their ROI for every dollar spent in marketing. It's become the "younger-looking skin" or "whiter whites" catch phrase in marketing presentations across the country. Who wouldn't want that? While all advertisers want to understand how their dollars are spent and allocate dollars to only the most effective strategies, I can't stress enough the need for marketers to use *judgment*. Predictive ROI and attribution models are a very, very imperfect science, sometimes masquerading as scientific truth. My best advice to marketers is to understand the assumptions and tweaks on which models are based. Many times, assumptions—often flawed—may determine results. So, not fully understanding them is very risky. I will explain.

Most marketers don't understand that the key objective of mathematical models is to reduce uncertainty surrounding a decision, not predict a precise outcome. They are often misapplied to forecasting specific results for which they were not designed. I was recently at a talk given by Steven Eriksen, a Babson College professor of modeling and simulation who put it bluntly: "Mathematical models or simulations are comprised of data and assumptions—both are wrong."

Before I get into the alternative technologies that are being sold to quantify the effect of ad campaigns in-market, I want to revisit the test-versus-guess dilemma.

THE TEST VS. GUESS DILEMMA

The pendulum has clearly shifted among marketers recently, who prefer to measure all in-market effects and predict results using attribution and marketing-mix models versus isolating specific variables and testing them in advance. In my view, this trend is a result of overzealous modeling firms pushing the results beyond their usefulness. But it is also a result of research companies not keeping up with technology.

The Research Lag

Let's be honest. The research industry and others involved in ad creative testing and many other forms of research have not been particularly innovative. They tend to do things the same way they did 40 years ago, and client-insight teams act as enablers because the practices are well-established, labeled as "best practice", and the budget approved. It's not that copy testing by big research firms is bad; it's just that it is far too slow and expensive to impact marketing decisions in today's world. It's like driving a gas-guzzling, rusted car from the '70s. It will still get you from point A to point B but not in the most efficient or effective way. Copy testing is disconnected from mix modeling, often done in different departments within the client. Marketers can learn the effects of their campaign from a marketing-mix model many months after the fact, hoping to better predict next year's outcome. But these effects are combined—simultaneous effects of creative, media, competitive activity, other marketing mix elements, etc.—and difficult, if not impossible, to disentangle. I am surprised at how much effort is put into trying to "fix" the old models rather than simply conducting an in-market experiment today.

There is a better way to understand advertising effects: test the various ad creatives separately using an approach to isolate only the creative effects. Then, test the ad in a live market and compare it to a matched control market that receives a different ad or no ad at all, keeping all other marketing treatment the same. This two-tiered testing approach allows a marketer to isolate the pure creative impact of an ad plus assess the in-market sales effect. Linking the creative drivers to in-market performance provides a quantification of ad quality.

It will always be better to isolate a variable and test it purely—keeping other things equal—than to try to extract it from a very complex model with simultaneous interactions. Either in a lab or in a controlled real-world experiment, comparing the test cell to the control cell—or pre compared to post—is just better in getting a precise estimate of the impact of the test variable by itself. "To get to the 'why' you need to be able to control things, and the only way to do that is within a lab environment," says Artie Bulgrin, senior VP of research and analytics for ESPN.

The lab environment allows for complete control of the variables being tested, which can be valuable in certain situations. Testing in a live market allows for a real-world impact, which also has its strengths and weaknesses. But the ability to test quickly and privately, with a consistent measuring stick, especially when compared with relevant competitive ads that are also running, is the best of both worlds.

Test Early and Test Often

Pretesting ad creative is not a replacement for marketing-mix models but a supplement, especially when the test results can be integrated into a holistic measurement plan including early-stage concepts or animatics through roughs to finished film. Having specific marketing response quantified from a test can inform the model with more precise response data resulting in far better predictive results than modeling alone. My advice to brands: "test early and test often" while developing their creative. Ad testing is faster and cheaper than it used to be, so more experiments can be designed to read specific effects or marketing treatments. Marketing-mix models are fairly blunt instruments evaluating overall spending levels and gross rating points (GRPs) and are not sensitive enough to evaluate specific variations between different ads. But they can provide comfort on the relative effectiveness of the elements of the entire national marketing plan. At Google, for example, the "test and learn" mantra rules. Internal teams are attuned to putting creative products in front of consumers and then, in real time, extracting insights through a cycle of testing, learning, and iterating. This is exactly how ad creative should be produced and fine-tuned more broadly. Marketers can know what works with certainty.

The test-and-learn cycle is ideal for marketing. Having a testing plan allows learning to be cumulative and avoids relearning the same thing next year. Testing early and testing often, giving the most weight to data that is most recent, and not giving too much credence to data that is in ancient historical databases enables advertisers to deliver the most impactful ads to their viewers and not "guess" based on last year's model.

As a famous economist once said, "All models are wrong; some are useful." Test and learn always beats guess and hope.

One thing is certain, that even if you are a great marketer, it is not always easy to predict how consumers are going to respond to a given ad. We have seen literally hundreds of examples of brands thinking something is going to work and then seeing it bomb spectacularly. Conversely, a brand may think something isn't going to work and then it takes off like wildfire, maybe even in a viral way. The philosophy should be: "Don't guess." The phrase "your opinion, while interesting, is irrelevant" applies to marketers deciding what creative is good or bad without viewer testing. It's the viewer's opinion that counts.

The marketing plan for today's brands should be built around a culture of experimentation—creating micro executions in multiple markets to create real-world experiments. Each unique market represents an opportunity to be a test or control market for a specific marketing variable, not just ad creative. Exclude markets from advertising and substitute with control ads. Apply coupons of different values to other markets. Change the media weight in some markets. Every market represents a different marketing execution. Market pairs can be matched on various criteria, or effects can be analyzed "pre-post" execution. The best companies have a master-testing blueprint for all complex campaigns. The resulting insight is unparalleled and can be incorporated into the marketing mix models. It's about creating your own relevant data by controlling specific and isolated variables rather than attempting to disentangle the effects happening simultaneously—this is when data is power (not to mention proprietary).

When considering varying ad creative, you need not have to just work with your agency to develop alternatives. Often your Agency of Record might be too wedded to a particular ad strategy. But in today's production environment, there are dozens of production companies that can produce test ads. This emerging countertrend of small, independent producers, the so-called "pop tent producers" (think YouTube), who are willing to produce an ad on the cheap. They have a high-definition camera and, before you know it, they're shooting a commercial and uploading it online. Ads from these new, unfamiliar sources might be great, highly creative, and indistinguishable from high-quality productions, or they might be terrible and damage the brand. A quick test of the work would mitigate the risk of a brand venturing into this world and having to retreat. Testing is integral to the strategy. Think of Dorito's ads for the Super Bowl; many are produced this way.

Even when taking the traditional approach, brands should embrace the ability to stay an extra half-day on the set and create several alternative cuts, and then, in post-production, change the music or the logo treatment or various post-production edits. All of this is relatively easy and low-cost and provides infinite testing possibilities. Some innovative brands are starting to take this test-and-learn approach to creative development and test nine or ten different executions.

Experimentation is getting easier with technology. It allows you to make modifications to the creative, which would have before taken weeks or months to redo. In the digital world, different music, a different logo, and more can be added, all very quickly. The ability to test all these ad versions needs to be fast and inexpensive as well, but through this iterative "test and learn" process, the final product is close to perfect.

Chapter 14

MEASUREMENT:
WHAT ARE BRANDS TRYING TO ACHIEVE?

*I notice increasing reluctance on the part of marketing
executives to use judgment; they are coming to rely too
much on research, and they use it as a drunkard uses a
lamppost for support, rather than for illumination.*
—David Ogilvy

In the previous chapter, I discussed the importance of testing early
and testing often. In this chapter, I will tackle the various pieces of
the modeling pie that determine ROI. In short, this chapter should
help readers better define the "R" and "I" in ROI as well as understand the dangers of assumptions and historical data in modeling.

Today, most brands are carrying out some form of ROI or marketing-mix measurement on their marketing efforts. A number of industry associations are putting forth best practices for these tools. Bob Liodice, the CEO of the ANA, issued a measurement mandate to address what he and others described as a "woeful state of insight into marketing effectiveness." You would think from all the marketing by the measurement players that the holy grail of measurement is upon us. In practice, however, we still have a way to go. While all CMOs would love to walk into their CFO's office with precise and accurate ROI numbers for every marketing activity, doing so with today's tools can be risky without a clear understanding of how the numbers are computed. "It's what the model said" is not an answer. Yet many CMOs, who may be experts in brand strategy and communication, are less expert in analytical models and often trust the more quantitative people on their team—who are often incentivized on the program's success. This decision can wind up inadvertently being a career-risking move.

There are some common pitfalls marketers often make when measuring marketing ROI with attribution models, marketing-mix models and other forms of predictive-versus-experimental measurement. The biggest pitfall is not paying enough attention when it comes to the assumptions in the model. I liken this to making sausage. People like it but don't want to know how it's made. That's a huge danger. I've built marketing-mix models throughout my career and, as any modeler knows, modeling is not a precise science. Marketers need to ask the right question to identify potentially arbitrary assumptions and avoid making a decision on what they *think* is hard data when it is not.

Mathematical models work best when there are known inputs and a clear, measurable objective that needs to be solved. UPS, for example, uses real-time data to plan and adjust routes for drivers. This is a great use of data analytics: a known list of addresses and packages for drivers, optimized by distance, fuel, and traffic patterns. These are known inputs and outputs (e.g., minimize fuel cost and delivery route time). There is no "art" in this, you are solving for known factors. This is where predictive models shine. Every day with a new list of package addresses, possible routes, and updated traffic conditions, the model can solve for an optimal solution.

Unfortunately, marketing variables are far less precise. There is an outcome variable—sales—but the connection between sales and marketing stimuli is not always directly known. For example, it is unknown how long the effect of a marketing stimuli will have on increasing sales or how long it will take to initialize and effect. If a viewer sees a TV ad, when would you expect that to result in a purchase? One hour? One day? One month? In addition, there are many factors in most live markets that simultaneously could influence that outcome: maybe the TV ad, maybe the point-of-purchase display, maybe a coupon, maybe a temporary price cut, perhaps its consumers' prior experience with the product, or maybe it's all of the above. Every one of these factors needs to be estimated, usually a priori, to allow the model to try to solve. But you can see the differences between the UPS example and the marketing example. In marketing, there is just not as much certainty.

The story of the emperor's new clothes comes to mind: Few people in the crowd want to call out questionable ROI computations for fear of jeopardizing their jobs. But the truth is that these models are just that—models—and models such as these, with many moving parts, are extremely fragile. There is a reason that real-world human trials are done between test and control groups when testing the efficacy of a new drug. There simply is no way to simulate all the various simultaneous environmental factors. It is much more valuable to compare results between live test and control groups than to simulate and predict them.

DEFINING AND PROVING ROI

The Customer Manufacturing Group, a marketing consultancy, conducted a study of current marketing ROI practices for the ANA. The study reported: "We believe that what passes for marketing ROI these days is not really true marketing ROI but something else—something related and possibly useful, but not, in fact, true marketing ROI." The industry is not even sure that ROI is the right metric. Many marketing expenditures are expenses, not "investment". They are not balance sheet items. Some have suggested simple incremental revenue minus incremental expenses, which sounds simple enough. Determining what revenues and expense items go into computation are the challenge.

The fact is, most marketing-mix models today are focused on ROI for specific marketing communications. Usually the "R" is some kind of lift measure—some incremental sales effect for example that the model assigns the marketing action. As we have discussed, this is an estimate given the simultaneous interactions. So while there are questions about the "R" in ROI, there are also questions about the "I". Many debates ensue about what costs should be included in the investment denominator. Decisions about what costs to include have a material effect on the outcome. Often an ROI estimate can improve simply by removing certain costs—costs for example that might impact a program's success, such as other marketing functions, marketing research, customer acquisition, or other program costs. Add to this the fact that in many organizations the program manager, who is often directly incentivized on the ROI performance, is in charge of computing it.

DATA INTEGRATION CHALLENGES

Even if the marketing communication ROI *per se* is to be measured, it still isn't simple. First of all, the input data is not available from one single source. The math behind multivariate regression modeling has been around for decades and is not the hard part of putting a mix model together. Various flavors of modeling design have emerged depending on the data inputs or simulations conducted. But the hard part is not the modeling; it's integrating all the data inputs. The modelers must collect, aggregate, and align all the various data elements (GRPs, spend data, sales data, other marketing data, pro-motions, pricing, creative data, manufacturer cost data, competitive data, etc.). Just getting the data to align by time and product can be a big challenge and take weeks. For a large national brand, the modelers collect and input literally hundreds of different marketing programs and try to relate those stimuli to sales. These disparate input data elements often have different lag times, periodicity, and so on. Some digital inputs can be populated in near-real time, while other elements might take weeks. Digital might have second-by-second reporting, whereas TV ad spending might be monthly versus four-weekly. Some inputs might be weekly but have end dates as Sundays versus Fridays. Some spending might be for the entire brand (e.g., Nissan) while other elements might be for a specific sub-brand

(Nissan Leaf). Some are measured in dollars spent, others in terms of reach, such as GRPs. Then, there is the dependent variable. If it is sales, how frequently is that reported? After a viewer is exposed to an ad, is there any lag before a sales lift? For fast-moving consumer goods, that lag might amount to a few days, but for automobiles, it might amount to years. You get the idea—data integration is a huge, labor-intensive pain.

Once all data elements are in a large time-series database, modelers can start creating their first models to look at relationships. They try to account for seasonality and other effects. Usually the results are often terrible in the early iterations. They really don't predict anything, and, in fact, the marketing elements often have a negative correlation to sales. What may be surprising to marketers is that many of the marketing effects are estimated by modelers first, not actually generated from the model itself.

THE DANGER OF ASSUMPTIONS

Generally, it takes modelers a lot of time to tweak the model and iterate, making new and different assumptions as they go. Some of those assumptions have a material effect on the result. For example, not too long ago I was with a client who had three unique TV ads in a campaign. The client determined the first ad was far better than the other two of the same campaign. Our data showed that the ads performed pretty much equally well. I asked the research team how they could have concluded that one ad was better than the other two when they were running the ads simultaneously with equal media weight (i.e., consumers had an equal chance of seeing Ad One, Ad Two, and Ad Three). In addition, they were reading the ads' effect on the store's sales data, and they didn't really know which ads each consumer saw. How could they know that Ad One worked better than Ad Two or Ad Three? Of course, they couldn't. The modeler had made a simplifying assumption that the majority of the incremental sales (two-thirds) would be allocated to Ad One and the remaining one-third would be split between Ads Two and Three. This was a purely arbitrary decision. These types of assumptions happen all the time and are the dark secrets of the modeling industry. It doesn't mean the choices are wrong, necessarily. It just means that, in some instances, the models aren't determining the result. The results can be arbitrarily assumed. The advertiser was ready to heavy-up the weight on the first ad and drop the other two creatives as justified by the model results, which would have been a mistake.

The principle of the Occam's razor theory is that among competing hypotheses, the one with the fewest assumptions should be selected. According to *Wikipedia*, other, more complicated solutions may ultimately prove correct, but in the absence of certainty, the fewer assumptions made, the better. Testing, for the most part has no assumptions. You are simply isolating one variable, executing in one cell, and comparing to a control cell.

EVERYTHING HAPPENS AT ONCE!

Marketing-mix models have a very difficult time accounting for simultaneous effects. If things happen simultaneously in your marketing, and there are no data points where each element behaves in isolation, it is very difficult to say which marketing variable accounts for which sales effect. You have to have very big differences in execution levels to be able to see it in the model results. Most of the time, they're kind of all running together, and the model makes allocations based on criteria that are usually assumed, such as the dollar size of the input.

These allocation models are designed to separate baseline sales (sales that would happen without marketing) and incremental volume due to specific marketing tactics. The key is to have enough variation in the data—both the inputs and outputs. I have seen cases in which sales were flat throughout the model period but there were very big differences in marketing execution. Trying to sort out any predictive relationships to sales when there is no variation is a modeler's nightmare.

DISTINGUISHING BETWEEN SHORT-AND LONG-TERM PERFORMANCE

Modelers also have a difficult time handling short-term and long-term marketing effects in the model. Some activities are to drive short-term sales and others are to drive long-term brand objectives. Communications need to be evaluated on what the advertiser was trying to achieve in the first place. All ads have short- and long-term impacts. But if returns are measured using a time frame that is too short, the real impact of the campaign might be undervalued. Brands that are repositioning may take years to be successful. Take Old Spice, for example. This is an old brand that most people associated with Grandpa's soap on a rope or Father's Day gifts. But this brand has been transformed over the past five years or so through youth-oriented campaigns and breakthrough creative. If these campaigns were held to a short-term ROI, they may have been considered unsuccessful. The brand had to stay the course to ultimately get the long-term positioning and sales impact it was after.

DANGERS OF USING HISTORICAL MODELS FOR PREDICTION

Prediction is very difficult,
especially if it involves the future.
—Niels Bohr

It's important to remember that the mix model's purpose is to explain and find relationships from past circumstances to reduce uncertainty of a future decision. The past will never be repeated precisely in every marketing and environmental condition. In fact, *all* will change, and the effects will largely test the model's ability to predict. Most models don't even assess the past precisely, relying on many tweaks and various assumptions. So how can they predict the future precisely? The fact is they can't, but they are often used as if they can. The best use for these models is as a rough explanation for what happened, not as a predictor of future behavior.

In addition, many companies fall into the trap of relying too heavily on their own historical data. Some companies have consumer data going back decades. Because of the investment to collect and store, and because it is easily accessible, many companies become too focused on history when it may no longer be relevant. I'm reminded of the story of Barack Obama's pollster when he and Hillary Clinton were vying for the Democratic presidential nomination. He was presented with polling data going back over a hundred years. Given the unique situation of an African-American candidate and a female candidate, he simply threw it all away. Just because the data is available, doesn't mean it is relevant today.

Insight teams for large brands often become enamored with their own data and often consciously choose to ignore more relevant and current data streams. Integrating new data streams is often avoided because they can present divergent signals that would challenge previous conclusions or provide alternative explanations. But better data is sometimes not found in historical databases but in new, faster, more relevant sources. The analysis might get messy with multiple, unpredictable data sources, but it is the only way to uncover the truth and the insight.

CREATIVE QUALITY: AN IMPORTANT BUT LESSER-USED INPUT

Ad creative quality, which we have explained as a key, measurable driver of marketing success is overlooked in most models. But even when creative is taken into account, creative used in the next year's campaign will likely not be identical to that of the modeled year. It could be good or bad, but it will be different. If a brand comes up with a radical new campaign, the prior year's model results are useless. Therefore, it's important to put in new creative scores, when they are available, to simulate the response. Recent successful models that relate advertising quality to sales growth do exist, but this relationship is often a longer-term effect. One recent such study published in the *Journal of Advertising Research* by Charles Young and Adam Page reports that "quality of advertising creative is a major factor driving sales response. Marketing-mix models attempting to quantify ROI are incomplete if they do not include a creative-quality variable."

Young and Page conclude that "relative performance of advertising versus the competitive set may provide insight into fundamental questions facing brand marketers" but are usually ignored in predictive models.

But even if creative is factored into the model, many marketers expect direct linear relationships between improved creative and sales. It is very difficult to simulate a media campaign and *only* vary the creative aspect. In addition, marketers often have unrealistic expectations on the role of creative in driving short-term sales lift. Creative can't solve everything, but that doesn't mean it isn't effective.

MODELS:
NOT WRONG BUT NOT PRECISELY RIGHT

As I mentioned earlier, it's not that the models are not right; it's that they are not *precisely* right. When there is a mathematical relationship, or when decisions are based on simplistic assumptions, care is especially prudent when using such a model for forecasting or predictive applications. The marketing-mix model simply tells you what happened and what seemed to work to explain the sales behavior of the previous year. It's not telling you that the same tactics are going to work in the current year, except at a very high level (i.e., of being "vaguely right"). This year you may have totally different creative. The competitive activity might be different. It's a big, complicated world out there, and it's simply impossible to account for all the different variables influencing your consumers. All models will spit out a number, but brands need to realize that they have a very high beta (i.e., of being "precisely wrong").

To paraphrase an industry executive at Ad:tech, who chose not to be identified:

> "Have you ever wondered why it is that Dynamic Logic tests and Vizu Brand Lift metrics always show lift to advertisers? Isn't this just a little surprising? Or why campaign analysis done by Google or Facebook on behalf of their advertisers are always positive? The studies and models are designed to provide a specific outcome, not to represent reality. But clients eat it up, so they are provided with rosy ROIs and lift metrics to run into their boss's office to justify their position. Even CMOs buy into these, touting such metrics in marketing plans and budget meetings. However, there is one problem. The numbers are often inflated. Unduplicated reach numbers, inflated. ROI numbers, inflated. We live in the Madoff marketing world where everyone wants to believe rather than ask the hard questions or look at the data themselves. If you are a CMO, I'd ask everyone in the organization if they are practicing Madoff marketing analysis, and tell them to show me the data."

The point of all of this is to make marketers aware of the dangers of overly simplistic measurement of a very complex marketing world. Measuring creative effectiveness, together with overall advertising campaign success requires setting clear objectives for the analysis: what costs/benefits are included and allocated, how specific marketing variables are going to be isolated and measured, and which testing variables and programs will be identified.

ROI quantification of marketing spending will continue to be a marketer's most important priority, as well as their Achilles heel. The models are improving over time, with improvement in the inputs. Some modelers are better than others. Some data inputs are better than others. Teams will constantly push the envelope of mathematical reason. Data quality will get better and more integrated. An increased proportion of marketing budgets will be spent on digital, where more data exists. More measured linkages between exposure and action will also improve models over time, but we shouldn't assume that the problems have been solved today. Marketers need to be informed.

The Customer Marketing Group goes even further: "The most radical, yet sensible, suggestion that we can make is that marketing ROI, while increasingly popular, is the wrong place to focus attention."

Experienced business professionals know that optimizing marketing communications will not necessarily increase sales immediately. In other words, just because you have created an effective marketing mix model with optimal ROI does not mean you are investing in the right areas, since you are only evaluating the ones chosen the previous year. Measuring what you did the previous year is based on a limited set of choices and doesn't mean you did the right things in the first place. Without testing each one, you have no knowledge on how successful alternatives might have been. It's an expensive way to learn. Determining the right activities by systematically designing experiments to test them is a better approach to improving marketing effectiveness.

Every measurement technique has its strengths and weaknesses. And every CMO is under pressure to prove value for the amount invested. It's crucial that marketers play an active role in determining analysis guidelines for the marketing scientists to follow. Where things are precisely measurable, measure them that way. When things cannot be measured precisely, test them in a way that allows them to be measured precisely. And retain a healthy dose of skepticism. Don't try to model the unknown. Instead, set up your experiment blueprint to find out the answers.

Chapter 15

ATTRIBUTION MODELS AND OTHER DIGITAL SURPRISES

We tend to overvalue the things we can measure
and undervalue the things we cannot.

—John Hayes

Attribution models, traditionally used by digital marketing, analyze data based on consumers' cookies and web behavior to determine which marketing action should get the credit for the consumer action, usually a purchase. It started with a fairly simple-minded "last-click" approach that gave 100 percent of the credit to the last marketing stimuli prior to the purchase. In other words, researchers theorized that the consumer's last interaction was what caused the sale. For example, if a consumer saw a digital banner ad for AT&T,

clicked on it, and came back later that day to buy a phone, that inter-action would get a tremendous amount of weight as the cause of the purchase. It's not a bad idea in theory if the only stimuli were digital and the consumer only saw that last impression. But it quickly breaks down with today's complicated multichannel marketing executions. I've actually attended meetings where people have said, "Hey, that Facebook post on that F-150 really caused that purchase to happen." But this goes against all reason regarding how purchases are actually made. Nobody's buying an F-150 based on a Facebook post or a banner ad alone.

Further, in some cases, that last impression getting the credit for the conversion or sale may not have even been viewed. Brian Weiser, from Pivotal, a New York-based advertising analysis firm has this to say:

> **The common use of simple attribution models makes the ad fraud problem worse.** *"Last-viewed" attribution—a commonly relied-upon approach connecting a desired marketing objective such as a site visit to the serving of a specific impression on a web page—may be contributing to ad quality problems too. For example, an ad at the bottom of a web page may never be viewed, but as the last ad to load, it may get all of the credit when a consumer eventually visits an advertiser's website.*

Attribution modeling has since improved somewhat. Attribution models can now attribute the marketing effect across a broader array of stimuli, some more precisely than others. They can now look at users' other activities and visits. The biggest drawback with these approaches is that you still don't know what you don't know. The models attribute behavior to what can be measured easily but either ignore or guess about the effects of other marketing elements such as TV ad or in-store promotion that isn't directly measured. Research shows that TV ads actually have a greater impact in driving online sales, but because the attribution models originally only looked at digital marketing, many brands have made the mistake of regarding digital marketing as the *only* marketing that is necessary.

Today, attribution models try to factor in TV and other offline advertising, but they tend to be underrepresented and poorly integrated. As stated in the quote at the beginning of this chapter, "We tend to overvalue the things we can measure and undervalue the things we cannot." Attribution models that I have worked with clearly overvalue the digital components that are easier to measure. In addition, many program managers are personally incentivized on the success of their programs—unfortunately, the reality is that the data that puts their programs in the best light typically becomes the data that is used.

Marketers make bad decisions when they cut some of their TV advertising or reduce their broad-based awareness brand advertising solely because they can't see immediate results in an attribution model. Of course, they only make this mistake once if their sales fall dramatically. Pepsi found this out the hard way a couple of years ago, surrendering base Pepsi market share to Diet Coke for the first time in history after slashing its marketing budget for everything except social media.

The analytical challenge comes when marketers put extra weight on the things they can measure the most precisely. A hundred different things may motivate consumers to buy a truck: a TV ad, past experience with the brand, a recommendation from a friend, a test drive, a print ad they saw in *Sports Illustrated*, a Facebook post, a digital ad, styling and the product itself, or recommendations from friends or family—a combination of many factors.

The correct attribution is almost impossible to determine precisely—it is not often even known at the individual consumer level. Because of this, most attribution models for complex multi-channel campaigns actually estimate the impact of each component first, rather than try to read them after the fact. Some firms will even ask the marketers what weight they should put on each factor.

From a recent publication from Adobe, leaders in attribution modeling:

> *"A successful attribution program requires stakeholders be well educated about what is and isn't possible. The goal of attribution is to get a better understanding of how marketing channels influence your customer's behavior, but this will never be a perfect understanding. Having these discussions upfront can ensure that realistic expectations are set and that the project isn't later judged a failure against impossible standards."*

With TV, you can't guarantee that the consumer was in the room watching your commercial. There's a pretty high likelihood, but you can't guarantee it. Then it's even harder to prove that that ad exposure triggered a response that lead them to purchase the product. With digital, you know if a consumer clicked on or hovered over an ad and took some action, and you can link that action to an online purchase.

But this doesn't mean the other, nondigital elements aren't effective and didn't contribute to that purchase decision. They could be far more effective, just harder to prove.

Attribution models work best if marketers can measure the entire purchase experience directly from start to finish. Online retailers, for example, can track from early top-of-the-funnel exposure through to purchase and all intermediate steps in between. But if a business has a large portion of their marketing and/or a large portion of their sales occurring outside digital, the models can quickly fall apart. The further away from a purely measured environment, the more guess work ensues.

To be fair, there are companies making strides in successfully linking cookie data to real-world purchasing. Data Logix, recently acquired by Oracle, can link cookie data to a person's frequent shopper card data to start to link ad exposures to purchasing. While these projects can still take some time to execute, and are not perfect, they represent solid, non-assumption-based linkage of exposure data to result data.

FRAUD ALERT

The promise that digital precisely measures a person's activity may not actually be that precise. Problems with identity systems that depend on cookies are widely known. Worse still, it is possible that the ad you bought and paid for was not even seen by a human. Recent studies, including one by White Ops, a digital consultancy, estimated that at least 25 percent of all video impressions are fraudulent: the ads are viewed by bots. *Twenty-five percent of them!* Some estimates from the IAB put the number even higher. The report found big-name companies, including Ford, Intel, MasterCard, and Wendy's were scammed by online fraudsters who have hacked the computers of millions worldwide. White Ops estimates that audience numbers at affected sites were inflated by between 5 and 50 percent. Further, since fixing the problem would result in considerably less ad revenue for publishers, most have been slow to respond.

On the topic of fraud, Bob Lidioce, CEO of the ANA, said, "I have had my eyes opened, and it's frightening." So frightening that it's hard to imagine any industry continuing to accept it. If a business bought and paid for 1,000 lawn mowers but only received 750, it would most likely scream or file legal action. It's only a matter of time until brands wake up and realize the scale of the problem and the fact that they are being scammed by the same companies that claim to be protecting them.

The trust initiatives by comScore, Google, and others in conjunction with the Interactive Advertising Bureau (IAB) seem to be seriously attacking the digital side of fraud in ad exposure and audience measurement. But it's hard to imagine a brand trusting a company that has been deliberately and knowingly overbilling them for fake impressions.

Video has been particularly hard hit by fraud because video ad units generate much higher CPMs. As a result, digital video has attracted the bot fraudsters on a massive scale, and more sophisticated fraud technology has resulted in a higher percentage of fraud than display ads.

In addition to bots, ads that run "below the fold" on a web page have, historically, been billed as viewed impressions when they were not seen. Google's Bob Arnold has written, "Recent Google research shows, among other things, that 56.1 percent of all served ad impressions (display and video) are not seen. Metrics mean nothing (or, should I say, reveal nothing) if an ad isn't seen. A new measurement metric, the viewable impression, now gives marketers better insight into whether people actually saw their ads." For all the criticism of TV, at least you absolutely know the ad ran, and the audience numbers have been independently verified.

The ANA calculates advertisers will lose $6.3 billion in 2015 to so-called bot fraudsters. Brands pay as if their ads were viewed by real consumers. Bill Duggan, ANA group executive vice president, said, "The survey confirms a deep, dark fear that people know is out there. Digital is supposed to be this great new accountable thing, but if we know it's not reaching the right people, that money is wasted."

Publishers might not even know their traffic is fraudulent, as bots have become more sophisticated to mimic human web behavior. But publishers are often reticent to change, given that they benefit from higher traffic and rates, at least in the short term.

Video is more expensive than display advertising and is growing fast. Because prices are higher, criminals can make more money with a smaller number of bots.

All this might seem tangential to the measurement of creative quality. But these are central issues that factor into marketing measurement decisions. The bottom line is that digital having perfect data is a myth, so having precise measurement of the effect is also a myth. As Google has said, their first priority is to measure ad quality from a fraud perspective. A close second priority is measuring ad quality from a creative perspective. Just because you are running a digital campaign does not mean the metrics are precise and valid. Measurement of all these elements triangulate into effectiveness measurement. They become inseparable in that quest and should have the goal of pointing in a certain direction, not yielding a precise answer.

So, while identifying tests to quantify individual elements is the most precise way to measure the effectiveness of the marketing variable, mix models still provide an aggregate estimate that is useful. The ARF suggests four key building blocks for effective ROI measurement using mix models: 1) comparable cross-platform GRP metrics (to understand how effective the ad delivery is), 2) incorporation of creative quality scores in models, 3) decision-timed measurement (meaning the measurement has to happen in time to influence the decision being made), and 4) collaboration versus hunkering down.

This is a good framework for marketers to incorporate in their modeling. GRP measurement of the ad delivery has improved to measure challenging outlets such as out-of-home or cross-platform (multiscreen) viewing. But the link between GRPs and sales also must incorporate the quality of the creative. Gayle Fuguitt, CEO of the ARF, says, "We know that great effective advertising is driven 75 percent by great creative and 25 percent by media plans," but most advertisers do not yet incorporate creative scores into their models.

The other key element identified by the ARF is timely preparation of the results. Too often, as mentioned before, results of ROI analysis come back too late to influence the outcome.

Chapter 16

COMMON PITFALLS FOR MARKETERS WHEN CREATING AND MEASURING ADVERTISING

Stopping advertising to save money is like
stopping your watch to save time.
—Henry Ford

We live in an unprecedented time for marketing. McKinsey refers to it as "marketing's golden age." But the golden age is not completely here yet, and although it might be coming, for most companies, it is a bit oversold. What is here is an age when data and science are converging quickly to provide marketers with real-time information. The concern is how much signal is in that data and whether the signal is the right one to begin with. Marketers need to challenge their data analysts and ask: "Do you really know that, or do you just *think* you know that?" If there is no proof, marketers need to tell their teams to produce proof through experimentation. They can improve their odds of success by avoiding some common mistakes. I have found the following are mistakes commonly made by marketers.

MAKING SMALL CHANGES AND EXPECTING BIG DIFFERENCES IN RESPONSE

Brand marketers spend most of their waking hours focused on a particular brand. It is natural for them to overanalyze things and even go beyond what consumers can perceive. Many times, these teams think that these small, virtually imperceptible changes will have a big consumer impact. As consumers, we know they don't. So why do marketers stop thinking like consumers?

Early in my career, I worked with a soda company that was considering a different style of lid for its can. Where the top of the can meets the side, there's a slight angle of about one-quarter inch. The brand was considering whether that angle should be smooth or have three small indentations, like steps. The brand team wound up spending half a million dollars to test which format performed better. Not surprisingly, consumers 1) didn't care and 2) could hardly see the difference when they held both cans in their hands, let alone tell the difference when standing in the shopping aisle. Marketers obsess about and overanalyze many things on which customers place little value. It was obvious that whatever choice the brand made, it wasn't going to impact sales. Ultimately, it comes down to common sense. Some things you just do without overthinking.

Another example comes from my experience with Miracle Whip. Years ago, that brand put a little plastic strip over the lid of the jar as an indicator of tampering. The company spent a ton of money testing the sales impact of the plastic strip. Not surprisingly, there was no difference between the test cells and control cells. That didn't mean that the added safety measure was a bad idea for the brand, but they expected it to drive sales directly/immediately.

Ad creative is often like that. Sometimes brands/agencies change creative just for the sake of changes without understanding that the impact is very minor. Ace Metrix is often asked to test two ads that our fingerprinting technology flagged as more than 94 percent similar—so similar, in fact, that most consumers could not detect the differences (usually a slight frame adjustment lasting about a second). Despite warning the brand team that the two similar ads will not score significantly differently when tested, the team will inevitably want to go ahead and test. Despite our view that testing is almost always a good idea, ads do need to be meaningfully different so consumers can respond to them. The results of the ad tests showed nearly identical results for both ads. This proved that these minute changes could not be detected by viewers. Ads with such subtle differences that the consumer cannot even perceive are simply not going to have a big impact on performance. Many brand managers stop thinking like consumers. The art of great marketing is not only to think like a consumer but also to be one.

Consumers often get brands confused, for example, if they see various brands promoting similar food. Many weight-control brands have recently broken away from the pattern of featuring celebrities, because consumers couldn't remember if Marie Osmond appeared for Weight Watchers, Jenny Craig, or some other brand. The new campaigns for these brands have become much more original, one for Weight Watchers even running in the 2015 Super Bowl. New creative ideas don't always work, but that's when pretesting can inexpensively shed light on potential breakthrough, game-changing ideas. Testing the same ad over and over and expecting a different consumer response is the marketers' definition of insanity. The recommendation: Go big or go home. Small tweaks are usually not noticed by consumers, and imitating the competition's campaigns results in brand confusion.

MAKING ASSUMPTIONS WITHOUT TESTING (UNDERTESTING)

In the first pitfall, we discussed overtesting: using very similar treatments and expecting big differences in consumer reaction. What is equally interesting is that some marketers don't do enough testing (or any testing). Sometimes, the same marketers undertest *and* overtest!

A recent example was a personal experience with Virgin America's new credit card. I applied for the card since I travel on the airline frequently. I changed over most of my automated payments to the card. About a month in, the marketing team informed the cardholders that we didn't like the look of the card and reissued it with a faint pink stripe on the side of the card. Who cares? But what I did care about was the unintended consequence that the reissued card now had a new expiration date, and none of the automated payments or stored card transactions worked—a big pain compared with a small benefit from a consumer perspective. How difficult would it have been to do a quick user survey and ask users about their card aesthetics and cost of switching cards?

Undertesting ad creative is commonly a result of the cost or time constraints of traditional copy testing. Traditional pretest companies can charge $30,000 or more for just one ad and take several weeks to get results. Most brands simply don't have the time or budget to test all of their ads in a campaign and often will test just one (usually, the 30-second spot). While an ad campaign will probably include multiple versions of a single ad (e.g., the campaign might comprise one 60-second ad and four different 15-second ads), the brand only tests one of them. Brand marketers feel they are doing their creative due diligence by testing, but they are not if they test just one execution.

Not testing all the executions is a big, big risk. I encourage brands to test all the different versions of an ad, and when we do, we sometimes find large differences, often because 15-second ads are much harder to execute well. It's clear that a 15-second spot, while cost effective from a media perspective, often misses the mark creatively and fails to deliver the correct message.

Consider this example from a recent Google campaign: When Google launched its Nexus 7 tablet, it broke a 60-second ad featuring a father and son camping in the backyard. The ad, which informed viewers of the tablet features while engaging in a touching scene, scored well. It was a top-quintile ad in the technology category.

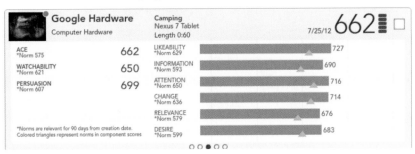

Figure 47

However, after running the 60-second spot, the company switched to a 15-second, cut-down version. This version just showed the father and son watching a movie on the tablet.

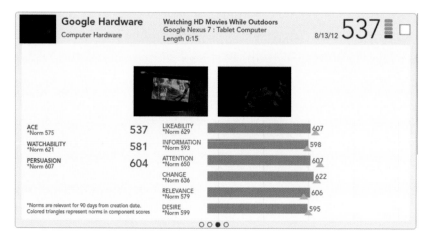

Figure 48

Not only did the cut-down ad not score well (bottom quintile), it also angered some viewers. "Bad dad" was one of the comments, along with viewers telling the parent to "switch off" and "unplug" to spend quality time with his son.

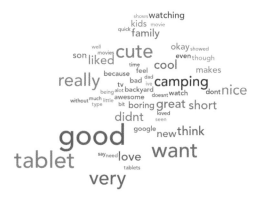

Figure 49

Google quickly responded with a different 15-second spot showing the father and son using the compass feature rather than

The Compass
Google Hardware   ACE SCORE: 575

watching a movie, which scored much better. This example proves the point that a strong, longer-form ad doesn't guarantee the success of a 15-second version of it.

Both P&G and Clorox have done a considerable amount of work perfecting the 15-second spot, the test result data. One of the highest-scoring 15-second spots of all time is a Clorox ad featuring a family bringing home every gross thing they have touched that day. As seen in the graphic below, its scores are impressive: it was in the 98th percentile in the funny category and, in 15 seconds, effectively communicated everything the consumer needed to know.

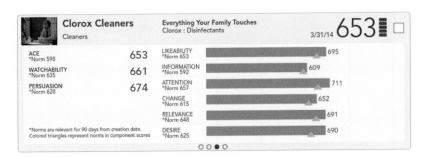

Figure 50

The trick with 15-second spots is to establish the point of the ad within three seconds. Otherwise, the ad spends too much time setting up, and by the time the ad is over, nothing has been com-municated. This obviously is much easier to do when viewers are familiar with the brand. It's not surprising that the best 15-second spots come from established brands or from an ad prompting an immediate stimulus, such as food/restaurant ads.

Another example of a successful 15-second spot is for Tide to Go, a portable stain remover. If you spill something on your shirt, you can just dab the remover on the stain, and you're good to go. The ad sets up the problem in three seconds. The woman in the ad says something like, "Oh, no, I ruined my shirt." A hand comes on-screen, dabs the product on the stain, and the stain is gone. It's Tide to Go Instant Stain Remover. This ad got the message across and delivered in 15 seconds. Tide didn't need a 30-second spot or a 60-second spot. The 15-second ad made excellent use of time.

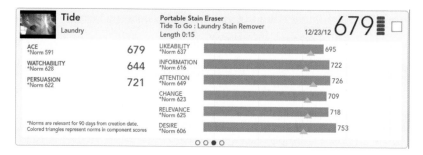

Figure 51

The table below summarizes how difficult it is to obtain a highly successful 15-second spot. Only 8 percent of 15-second spots have an Ace Score of 600 or better, while 12 percent of 30-second spots and almost 20 percent of 60-second spots score above 600.

	Ad Length	Ace Score Over 600	Ace Score Under 400
0	:15	8.4%	4.8%
1	:30	11.9%	3.0%
2	:45	9.3%	9.3%
3	:60	19.1%	5.4%
4	1:30	37.9%	2.3%
5	2:00	30.8%	5.1%

Figure 52

Clearly, it is much easier to tell a complete story if viewers have 60 seconds to work with. Of course, these longer-form ads also cost four times more to produce, so many brands opt for shorter spots. But, more often than not, 15-second spots don't perform as well as 30-second spots, and even 60-second spots don't always offer the right amount of time to get the advertiser's message across. This is why Google, which tends to be an innovator, started advertising with 90-second spots. Google's strategy was to tell a story, make viewers feel something, create a short film. The company's "Search On" TV spot was a retrospective of the most searched elements of 2014. It aired on New Year's Eve and was one of the most successful ads of the year, powered by extremely high scores in the categories of Attention, Likeability, Emotion, and Relevance. Google often follows the 90-second ad with "reminder" 15-second spots. But even Google is learning. For Chromecast, Google found that its 15-second ads were not as effective in delivering product information. In this case, the 30-second spot did a much better job of explaining the new product.

In some other categories a 15-second spot can work just as effectively as longer forms. We see this in casual dining ads in which a familiar brand's food can illicit just as strong an emotional response and Ace Score with a 15-second ad as a more expensive 30-second version.

The importance of the 15-second format in digital is becoming apparent. With viewers' ability to skip the ad after viewing certain lengths (five, seven, ten seconds, etc), it's critical to understand what elements need to be communicated in those first seconds to convince viewers to continue to watch through the end. But in the end, the message is the same: test every type of impression you plan to air.

MAKING MEASUREMENT MISTAKES

It's important that measurement criteria and methodology are established and understood prior to running the campaign. As mentioned in previous chapters, I have seen ROI pressure causing the attitude in which any number is better than no number. In these cases, computations and analyses are downright reckless. Some common mistakes are:

a) Overattributing marketing effects to the highest-measured variables, highest-spend variables

b) Incorrectly allocating marketing costs or allocating too much to specific marketing programs

c) Relying on prediction rather than empirical testing

d) Relying on attribution models that oversimplify the environment and buyers' actual behavior

This flawed practice is unfortunately widespread. Assumptions are made and not called out. Incorrect allocations and model tweaks are all made in the name of data science. ROI analysis, especially analysis of more challenging vehicles such as TV, should be done using defensible test vs. control data to reduce uncertainty in decision making, but even then, it will not achieve three-decimal-point precision.

BEING UNAWARE OF TARGETING FLAWS

We have all seen the examples of digital targeting run amok— where your online behavior results in being targeted by products or services that you are actually not looking for. For example, you complain to a company that they didn't ship your purchase on time. The product was out of stock, or worse, the company took your money and didn't send you anything. And so you're filling out a complaint form, and you're very aggravated. And guess what? Because you typed the name of that company, you are bombarded with retargeted ads for that company. How many times have you booked a trip and gotten ads for a month for the destination you just visited? Targeting can be infuriating.

Cookie-blocking technologies and privacy advocates predict the end of cookie-based tracking and targeting. Ultimately, if targeting and retargeting doesn't go away completely, its scope is likely to be curtailed. However, even if I don't delete my cookies, targeting snafus still exist in the system. In addition, traditional targeting often doesn't take into account the content on the page. Seeing an ad for Tide being displayed beside an ugly plane-crash news article is just one example of inappropriate targeting.

Not to mention the duplication in reach associated with different ad networks targeting the same individual with different cookies. Digital advertisers often pay multiple ad networks for unique reach. But it is more common that these two vendors are delivering to the same people twice, not twice the number of people. The ad networks often use the same cookie clearing house vendors (DMPs). All of these double-counting issues, whether involving fraudulent impressions or duplicated counts of unique people viewing, will be resolved eventually, and many initiatives are underway to improve accuracy and ensure advertisers get what they think they are getting. But the issues aren't fixed yet by any stretch, and marketers need to be aware that the theory and math of the targeting algorithms are often flawed.

The moral of the story is that even if an ad is well-targeted doesn't mean the ad is effective. And further, just because your data came from digital does not mean it is without errors.

OVERFOCUSING ON A CORE DEMOGRAPHIC TARGET FOR A HIGH-REACH CAMPAIGN

An extension of this idea is the mistake some brands make of using high-reach vehicles to speak to specific targets.

Beer brands are notorious for testing their ads only against 21- to 25-year-old, beer-drinking males and many times wind up producing ads that are offensive to most women. When you see a Heineken or Budweiser ad, on the other hand, you're not offended, even if you're not a beer drinker. It's still an interesting brand impression. If you buy beer for family members who are visiting and enjoy beer, maybe that ad would influence your buying decision, especially if you were to compare it with another brand's ads that may be annoying or offensive in some way. Newsflash: women both drink and buy much of the beer consumed at home in this country, so why produce ads they hate?

Even big brands with great advertising can make mistakes. Mercedes is an interesting example. For a Super Bowl spot a few years ago, the company featured Kate Upton in a preliminary ad in which she was scantily dressed while a football team washes her Mercedes for her. It was intended to deliver a message of "girl power, women first, we're in control." But when we tested it, it had the complete opposite effect.

The Mercedes brand tends to perform well with females, with females representing a large part of the Mercedes buyer base. This ad would have been a disaster if they'd run it at the Super Bowl. By finding out ahead of time, Mercedes was able to replace the ad with a far more successful—and gender-neutral—ad that featured Willem Dafoe pretending to be the devil. And yes, Kate Upton was in that ad but in a totally different role that was not offensive to women.

It's simple to also test your creative on a general population sample, at the same time as a more targeted sample. It's an inexpensive way to make sure that even if the ad is targeted at a specific buyer segment that it doesn't have the opposite effect with other groups. With TV especially, it's just safer to assume that everyone is going to see it.

PAYING TOO MUCH ATTENTION TO SOCIAL MEDIA LUNATICS

As mentioned earlier, paying too much attention to social media signals can be dangerous. As an input, social media data can be useful. But as the sole source of viewer reaction, it is dangerous. Not only are those commenting on ads not typical viewers, but they often have a particular, usually somewhat negative, agenda. Just because social media is big doesn't mean it's unbiased.

In addition to the problem of representation, there is also a signal/noise ratio issue. For example, if you were to look for the brand "Outback" in a Twitter data stream, you would find tweets that have virtually no relationship to the brand ad that was aired. Overwhelmingly, the tweets are on lines of "I'm sitting here at the Outback," or even more generically, "I'm going out back." It's extremely difficult to align social media commentary with specific marketing stimuli in everyday situations (the Super Bowl being perhaps a unique outlier).

HAVING UNREALISTIC CREATIVE EXPECTATIONS (IT'S THE PRODUCT, STUPID)

Lest we forget, the importance of the product and the viewers' experience with it drive creative response; it's not the other way around. As Stephen Denny said, "If dogs don't like your dog food, the advertising doesn't matter." A good ad can't save a bad product or experience.

Many marketers I've worked with have an unrealistic expectation of what ad creatives can do. That's not to say creative is not important. It is. But a great ad can't make up for other product or marketing shortcomings. Further, a great ad campaign, if it is designed to reignite or reposition a brand, can take years to be successful. Rarely are these overnight sensations. Consumer attitudes change slowly and their behavior, even slower.

Based on scientific research and validated by our own data is the fact that the most important response to an ad is consumers' product/ brand perception. When HP launched its ill-fated Palm OS tablet late into the tablet market, after Apple and Android, its TV creative performed quite well. It was the product that couldn't defeat iPad or Android. While I am not suggesting that this ad campaign was a success—the product failed in the market—it clearly was not the only factor in determining what influences purchase, as is the case with most brands. In fact, this is empirically proven across all ads in the Ace Metrix database. This point has big implications for brands that have unrealistic expectations about what creative can accomplish and is why many ROI models that ignore product realities are doomed. It also has huge implications for small or less-familiar brands trying to develop new users.

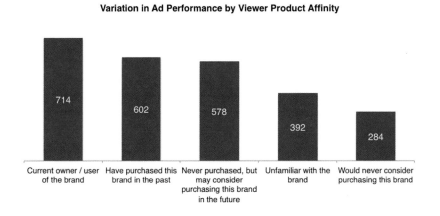

Variation in Ad Performance by Viewer Product Affinity

Figure 53: A consumer's personal experience with the brand can have significant effect on their reaction to an ad. Consumers who claim that they "currently use" an advertised product awarded an ad scores more than twice as high as those unfamiliar with the brand.

The above chart shows that viewers who say they "currently use" an advertised product give a score for the ad more than twice as high as viewers who say they are "unfamiliar" with the brand. That is a shocking difference and an interesting twist on the mere-exposure effect. (The mere-exposure effect refers to the phenomenon that repeated exposure to stimuli, over time, creates a positive emotional connection). This means that advertisers trying to reach consumers who are unfamiliar with the advertiser's brand must create an ad that breaks through and changes/informs those prospective users' perceptions—not an easy task. The recent Southern Comfort campaign, which featured some shocking and comical devices, succeeded at breaking through and grabbing attention of a new type of user.

The following table shows ads that scored highly amongst non-users of the brand. Typically, these ads are showing unique features and have an overall product orientation rather than a break-through story or high emotion. These brands are successfully using reason to convince non-buyers to change their consideration set. That is not the only way to successfully market to non-users but successful in the cases, particularly, when non-use is a function of awareness of the new product or feature.

Highest Scoring Ads Among Brand Averse

Brand	Ad Title	Ace Score
KitchenAid Small Appliances	Ignite Your Culinary Creativity	728
Kohler	Home Depot Whoa	723
Samsung Mobile Phones	Water Resistant	721
Kohler	Touch, Don't Touch	710
Hyundai Luxury Auto	(AUG) (SB 14) Dad's Sixth Sense	699
Hoover	Change That Changed Everything	693
Philips Small Appliances	Revolution in Healthy Cooking	688
Mazda Corporate Promotions	Braeden's Story	684
Samsung Mobile Phones	Makes Everyday Better	681
Dyson	Competition with Test Dust	675
Samsung Televisions	Curved	674
Hyundai Luxury Auto	(SB 14) Dad's Sixth Sense	668
Samsung Large Appliances	Easy Access to Foods	665
Breyer's	Parents Don't Want to Share	663
Maytag	Something Extra Inside	663
Ad Council	Deer	662
Clorox Laundry	Bleach This	662
Amazon Fire Phone	Fire Phone	659
Samsung Mobile Phones	Science Reality	659
Longhorn Steakhouse	Summer Taste	657

Figure 54 shows ads with the highest Ace Scores among viewers who selected "Would never consider", "never purchase but may consider", or "unfamiliar with the brand."

The importance of brand familiarity/product affinity is not a new concept. In fact, our data validates the Rosser Reeves fallacy from decades ago.

Rosser Reeves was one of the original *Mad Men* advertising gurus of the '50s. He based his thinking on his "questionable cause fallacy," a theory claiming that the existence of a correlation between A and B implies causation. He observed that consumers who are aware of an ad campaign are more likely to buy the advertised product. Most people credited high ad awareness with causing the purchase. However, as Reeves pointed out, brands with higher consumer awareness and product usage are more likely to create ad awareness than the other way around. People are more likely to pay attention to brands they are already familiar with and even seek out those brands' ads. As he said, "You must make the product, not just the ad, different." The role of the brand/product experience cannot be understated. A bad product cannot be fixed by a great ad.

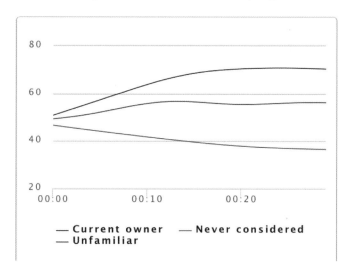

Figure 55: Ad performance based on the viewers product affinity.

In the above chart, the ad performed poorly (relative attention second-by-second is the vertical axis) among the "never-considered" cohort. Those viewers were four times more likely to skip the ad as well as pay less attention throughout. The data also shows that product affinity is far more important, but related to, demographic differences. An ad may be perceived well by 21–35-year-old women because they are familiar with and likely to use a particular product, not related to the demographic alone.

Other environmental factors exist as well. For example, the norms for automobiles, real estate brokers, and other large-ticket items scored markedly lower, leading into and during the recent recession. Receptivity to financial services ads decreased during the poor economy because many people were infuriated by Wall Street.

An example of the importance of product affinity in advertising effectiveness can be seen in the early P&G Olympics ads.

Originally, this campaign presented P&G as the "proud sponsor of moms," with the message that motherhood was "the hardest job in the world." These ads created a powerful emotional connection between moms and their young sports-minded children. There were two issues with the P&G ad campaign. First, the longer, two-minute version was able to develop the story of moms and their relationship with their kids much better than the 30-second ad, but the 30-second ad was all that ran on TV. Many people were, initially, confused by it. Second, most consumers related to the story but were confused by the P&G logo at the end. And the significant part of this kind of creative analytics is to show the importance of clearly relating the brand logo to the emotional ad message. Brands often try to establish an emotional connection between their products and consumers. In fact, a brand is often defined as the emotional or lasting memory of a product beyond its physical characteristics. P&G was quick to recognize that the umbrella corporation was much less familiar to consumers than its individual flagship brands (Tide, Pampers, Pantene, Head & Shoulders, etc.). So it adjusted the closing screen to display its product logos. One consumer stated, "I didn't know that P&G made consumer products."

INSUFFICIENTLY DEFINING
THE BRAND'S ADVERTISING OBJECTIVE

Many times, in discussions with brand teams and their agencies, there isn't a great deal of clarity on what the ads are specifically trying to accomplish. Often, the ad is trying to achieve too much (increase sales by 15 percent in March) or is poorly defined with vague language such as "build awareness." We like to challenge the teams to understand not just whom the ad is going to and what message is being delivered but also how the ad will affect viewers, based on what else they are being exposed to. Ads need to have a specific objective. They must have breakthrough quality (high Attention and Likeability), inspire product passion and loyalty, provide new and/ or specific product information, and so on. They should be targeted to a specific cohort: new users unfamiliar with the product, existing users the brand wants to encourage to buy more, and so on. Then, the concepts, storyboards, all the way to finished film can be tested against the specific criteria. Too often the objectives are either vague or overly precise (e.g., increase sales by 13 percent) and therefore suffer from the measurement challenges described earlier.

CONCLUSION

U ltimately, this book is about quality. The quality of creative and the quality of measurement matter a great deal. Quality matters to brands, agencies, and of course, the viewing public. Milton Hershey said, "Give them quality. That's the best kind of advertising." And the only way to improve creative quality is to measure it.

Going forward, I believe that systematic creative measurement, complete and ubiquitous, will change our industry. Quality creative is the highest driver of value in the ad business. It needs to be measured consistently so the value can be unleashed. Data is more readily available to inform all facets of the creative production and execution ecosystem than ever before.

But in a more specific sense, success of a campaign is also about matching the style of the creative to the brand objective. This requires an understanding of how the ad works with viewers, not just an overall pass/fail score. Producing ads people choose to watch and pay attention to is not an easy task. Producing ads that cause viewers to seek and share them is even harder. But measurement through experiments helps us to adjust and improve and know how the communication works and manage risk.

It wasn't easy for the industry to adopt a measurement mandate with respect to creative. "You can't measure art" is what I've heard over and over. But the truth is you can blend the science of measurement with creative art. And, to reiterate, we aren't measuring how creative the ad is but how successful it is. As Leo Burnett wisely said years ago, "You can measure an ad scientifically, but you can't create an ad scientifically." With any new technology, there is the Prince Machiavelli syndrome. You have all the detractors who benefit from the old system and merely lukewarm defenders of the new one. It's the same with anything that's truly innovative. A lot of people have a vested interest in doing things the old way. However, there are undeniable benefits to understanding creative success by measuring it.

It took a while for the industry to understand that agencies that produced the best work could get paid more by measuring creative quality and proving their value. And weaker work could be improved. Brands eliminated waste and produced results in time to have an impact and remove risk on an airing campaign.

If advertising quality improves, it's not a zero-sum game. Everybody wins. The viewers benefit because the ad is more appealing: something they choose to watch. The advertisers benefit because the performance is better in terms of sales or what they're trying to accomplish, and the agencies also benefit because, obviously, the better creative is getting rewarded. Digital publishers benefit because user experience is improved.

Everyone has heard so much, recently, about big data and marketing ROI, but few have reaped all the rewards. CMOs have tough jobs in today's world. They have to be experts not just in marketing and strategy but also in data science and technology. I've heard that some marketing teams are starting to spend more on technology than the Chief Information Officer does. A great deal is being spent on everything from marketing automation to programmatic ad buying and delivery and improvements in measurement. In addition, the volume of ads produced, particularly with user-generated content and social media are already increasing faster than brands can evaluate them. Small pop-tent producers are trying to get a piece of the brand budgets. There has to be systematic creative measurement that is fast and at scale so marketers assess success, potential, and downside risk of video creative before the ads air. Speed allows fast modifications to be made and then retested. These tools exist today but are often under-leveraged by marketers in favor or older, slower, but more familiar methods.

Marketers are under constant pressure to prove results to their CEOs. The recent McKinsey study of CEOs cited earlier reported that 75 percent agreed that "marketers are always asking for more money but can rarely explain how much incremental business this money will generate." This pressure can often translate into producing an ROI number, any number, without proper scrutiny of the methods. I hope marketers who read this book will take a second look at how their modeling suppliers operate and how their predications and analytics work. After all, it's the marketer's job that's on the line. Oversimplification of the measurement challenge is a pending danger.

I challenge marketers and researchers to embrace complexity. Data is everywhere, and its volume is exploding. In some cases, there's just too much data to make a decision, as opposed to years ago when data was scarce. But the right tools and judgment can simplify this complexity. Now, it's much more about selecting the right data from all the data that's available to inform the decision, or you can experiment and create your own data. Being intelligently selective is essential. In addition, conflicting signals abound, wih many data elements pointing in different directions. A common response is to ignore what doesn't agree with the hypothesis, but that is short-sighted. It's important for marketers to dig deeper with their research and for analytical teams to uncover what's really going on. As Einstein said, "Keep things as simple as possible, but not simpler."

To me, not wanting to test an ad before it goes on air is simply a matter of too much creative ego. Some agencies have contracts with clients who prohibit their ads from being tested. There is a misguided myth that measurement kills creative. Actually, the opposite is true— and most of our clients would agree that measurement of a performance of marketing success is absolutely essential in today's world. Marketers want to run ads that they know are going to be successful. Measurement, especially early on, can really help to make the small changes that make things work better. Don't forget that almost every year, during the Super Bowl, the most expensive advertising event in the world, a brand runs an untested ad and must apologize for it later—damage that takes years to undo.

It's also important to measure the impact of in-market forces beyond the ad itself. While it's important to measure the purely creative effect, it's also important to see what impact other variables, such as media weight, share of voice, and competitive activity have on the brand. Brand teams are often slow to learn that their sales can be just as affected by a competitor's creative quality. It's not just about looking at yourself. It comes back, again, to only knowing how good your advertising is if you know how good everybody else's advertising is. But knowing your ad creative is strong before it airs provides a huge advantage before jumping into the competitive fray.

Brands are embracing digital at an accelerating pace. The promise of better measurement is clearly one reason. The emergence of video is another. But as with any new system, there are kinks and realities that don't live up to a supplier's hype. Digital is not a panacea and requires hard work to reap targeting and measurement benefits and mitigate fraud and waste. It will get better over time, but it isn't perfect yet.

As a colleague recently said, marketers need to stop buying screens and start investing in the consumer journey. All-screen video is here to stay, and soon, all screens will have content and ads delivered digitally.

One brand we worked with evaluated its TV ads by looking at internal call-center data within an hour of airing the commercial. It was clear that some commercials were much more effective than others in generating call-center volume. Ace Metrix was able to identify and isolate a particular variable that drove the performance. As it turned out, it was not just the ad's high likeability and ability to grab attention that drove consumers to pick up the phone; it was also the fact that the ad was highly informative. Consumers had to gain enough product information to prompt them to call. Because that brand's marketers now knew which characteristics really drove the performance they wanted, they set them as a testing standard that an ad must achieve before airing. That's one of the most exciting thing we're doing with clients: testing and analyzing the data to know specifically what drives in-market performance. The same is true for programmatic players. We work with our partners to identify creative performance markers that can predict higher view-through rates or specific postexposure behavior, such as website visits, clicks, and so on. Once we know what metric drives performance, we can optimize against that metric.

The marketers' challenge has shifted from delivering the right message to getting consumers to pay attention in the first place. Advertising technology allows viewers the space to make a conscious choice—to view or not to view—and that will be the biggest marketing challenge of our generation. What can I do to ensure I get and keep viewers' attention? With so many competing forces vying for it, human attention is voluntary and limited, but great creative can unlock the door.

On the other hand, if marketers try to measure the creative component too precisely, or they try to get too formulaic in terms of what they think is going to work, the ads become too predictable. Ads from an assembly line don't break through. Viewers are conditioned to ignore or avoid them. The "safe" creative is usually the riskier strategy for the brand. It's still the role of the creative team to create, surprise, and delight, or inform; it's not the job of the viewer. But it is also the job of creative teams to listen to feedback and adjust if necessary.

Senior executives among our clients say that it's almost impossible to think about how they can get their arms around all of these different creative executions without understanding how their creative performed relative to all the competitive messaging. I remember seeing ads a few years ago, during the peak of the recession. Almost every automotive brand advertising promoted "zero percent financing" because the industry was in a slump. Then, relative newcomer Hyundai came out with an ad that announced, in a soft Jeff Bridges-like voice, "If you lose your job, we'll buy your car back." It was an incredible breakthrough ad, one of the highest-scoring ads of the year. It delivered a fundamentally different message: it was clear, people liked it, they paid attention, and it also scored high on Relevance and Information. When it aired, Hyundai experienced a big surge in popularity, and six months later, the company had a record sales quarter as a result of that campaign. The message is important, but also, how the message is told.

It might have been easier to write a book where I could jump on the modeling bandwagon and talk about a new ROI predictive model that we had created that could provide marketers with some magically precise ROI computations for every dollar spent. But to do so would be to ignore one of the most important fundamental truths about advertising—that creative matters. This book is about the use of data, together with marketing content experts to answer specific questions, rather than evaluate hypothetical outcomes from simulations. As I have said, I am not against the use of these predictive marketing models, I am against their misuse. Ultimately, it's the mathematical models that are the true commodity, not the ad creative. The engineers and data scientists, while necessary, don't understand the emotion behind marketing to people.

Every June, the Cannes Lions festival celebrates the pinnacle of the art of the creative. But recently, the event has expanded to include other innovation and technology categories. This is a microcosm of the entire industry, the coming together of science and art, of technology, creative, and innovation. The underlying purpose of this book is to inspire creativity in advertising and in measurement. Creativity is the way human beings move forward. To enable growth and improve quality and efficiency, creative measurement is a prerequisite. Creative quality matters. Creative rules.

INDEX